It's Time

# It's Time

## Explore Your Dreams and Discover Your Gifts

### Diane Noble

*Diane Noble*
*Zeph 3:17*

 **Baker Books**
A Division of Baker Book House Co
Grand Rapids, Michigan 49516

© 1995 by Diane Noble

Published by Baker Books
a division of Baker Book House Company
P.O. Box 6287, Grand Rapids, MI 49516-6287

Printed in the United States of America

### Library of Congress Cataloging-in-Publication Data

Noble, Diane
    It's time : explore your dreams and discover your gifts / Diane Noble.
       p.    cm.
    ISBN 0-8010-5155-X (pbk.)
    1. Empty nesters—United States—Life-skills guides. 2. Middle-aged women—United States—Life-skills guides. 3. Middle-aged women—United States—Religious life. I. Title
HQ1059.5.U5N63    1995
646.7'0082—dc20                          95-12361

Scripture is taken from the HOLY BIBLE, NEW INTERNATIONAL VERSION®. NIV®. Copyright © 1973, 1978, 1984 by International Bible Society. Used by per-mission of Zondervan Publishing House. All rights reserved.

*For Marihelen*

*Have I ever told you you're my hero?*
*You're everything I would like to be.*
*I can climb higher than an eagle.*
*You are the wind beneath my wings.*

LARRY HENLEY AND JEFF SILBAR

# Contents

# Acknowledgments

ithout the women who so openly shared their dreams, this book would never have been born. This work belongs to them. Many requested that their real names not be used so that their identities would be protected. I say to them all, "I thank my God every time I remember you. In all my prayers for all of you, I always pray with joy because of your partnership. . . . It is right for me to feel this way about all of you, since I have you in my heart" (Phil. 1:3–5, 7).

Special gratitude goes to my friend Paul Hawley, editing and theological advisor extraordinaire, for consultation and advice.

My deep and heartfelt thanks goes to my friend and colleague Jo Marie Dooley for the story in chapter eight that was born of her tender memories.

Perhaps my greatest thanks is last, that to my family. I thank my beautiful daughters, Melinda and Amy, whose preparations to fly from the nest created within me the need to look beyond those precious years of "hands-on" motherhood to dream new dreams of my own. And deep gratitude to my husband, Tom, whose love, support, and encouragement never waver.

# Prologue

We all have dreams. Most of us have more than one. As women, our dreams often include those we have for our children, our husbands, and our families. But what if, after all these years, we find there is time to dream another dream, one that is all our own?

We've been caught up in the day-to-day busyness of raising a family. Yet suddenly, the time and energy we've poured into the lives of our children and the running of our families are no longer required. We may find that we've lost sight of the dreams we once had.

Whether single or married, whether we've had a career outside the home or within it, our place in the world has suddenly shifted. It can be a time of feeling displaced or unneeded.

It can also be a time of great adventure.

This book is about exploring a world we may have forgotten about, or may have been too busy to notice.

It is about "enlarging the place of our tents and stretching our tent curtains wide" (Isa. 54:2, paraphrased) and seeing what God has for us during the next decades—the best decades—of our lives.

It is about having the time, at last, to nurture our own spiritual, emotional, and intellectual growth, to become all God intends for us to be.

It is about following our dreams.

It is about time.

Throughout this book there will be exercises that involve keeping a journal. Let me explain: The journal will be a personal record of your journey. You will dream dreams and pursue dreams. You will discover or rediscover things about yourself that will change your life.

Reading about change is good, but actively involving yourself is better. Involvement is the vehicle for change.

I suggest you purchase a 5 x 7 notebook or a bound blank-paged book (available in most bookstores). Open it to the first page and write:

> Enlarge the place of your tent,
>    stretch your tent curtains wide,
>    do not hold back;
> lengthen your cords,
>    strengthen your stakes.
>
> ISAIAH 54:2

Under it write: It's Time! (For *your name*)

# 1

# There's Finally Time for Me!

*There is nothing like a dream to create the future.*

VICTOR HUGO

*H*ey, Mom!" Kirsten's voice sounded tired, but excited. "I made it! I'm moved in."

Through the receiver, Linda heard the din of rock and rap and excited freshmen voices blasting through the halls of Kirsten's new dorm. "That's wonderful, Honey," Linda shouted, hoping her daughter could hear her voice over the chaos. "How was the drive?"

"It was great, Mom. It only took three hours and twenty minutes to get here. Then I found some guys to help me carry my stuff up to my room."

Smiling to herself, Linda pictured the "stuff." That morning, when Kirsten backed out of the driveway and blew her parents a good-bye kiss, her car had been loaded headliner high with clothes, shoes, stereo speakers, tapes, cowboy boots, CDs, rolled-up posters, a guitar, and an old, worn teddy bear. There had been little room left, even in the driver's seat, for Kirsten.

"What floor is your room on?" Linda pictured her daughter's knights-to-the-rescue trudging up dozens of stairs loaded with heavy boxes.

"The fourth, Mom," Kirsten said, laughing, as if she'd read her mother's thoughts. "But we've got elevators. No one broke his back."

Linda heard another burst of loud music, followed by a peal of laughter.

"Mom, I've gotta go," Kirsten yelled into the phone. "I just wanted you to know I made it."

"Sweetie, take care of your—"

"What—what?" Kirsten hollered, the background clamor again growing louder. "I'm sorry, Mom. I can't hear you."

"I said, 'I love you!'"

"Yeah. Me too." There was a short pause, then she added, "And, Mom, please don't worry. I'll be fine. I'm grown-up now."

Then the line went dead.

Linda returned the receiver to its base.

Suddenly the house seemed very quiet.

And empty.

And lonely. So very lonely.

For years her life had revolved around the activities of her children, Jeff and Kirsten. As of today, they were both gone. Jeff had married two years earlier, and now Kirsten, the family's baby, had just left home for college.

Linda poured herself a cup of coffee and sat at the kitchen table. She rested her chin in her hand. Absentmindedly, her fingertips began tracing the pen and pencil gouges on the table's worn oak top. Tears warmed her eyes as she remembered the little fingers that once held those pens and pencils, laboring over homework.

What memories that old table held! What tales it could tell of family love: the laughter and chatter accompanying the meals eaten together, the mealtime blessings uttered above chubby folded hands, the good-natured banter shared by friends eating pizza during a sleep-over.

Where had the time gone?

Linda's mind drifted back through the years. She remembered bringing Jeff home from the hospital. He'd been a miniature version of his father, with his dark hair and big, serious eyes. She'd rocked him, played with him, read to him, rejoiced in him. She'd wondered how God could ever create a more perfect and beautiful child. Then, just three years later, Kirsten arrived, round and pink, all smiles, light, and laughter. God had done it again!

The years raced by. Before she knew it, the children were in preschool, then grade school, then middle school. And Linda's life became a whirlwind of Little League, ballet and piano lessons, soccer, gymnastics, drill team, cheerleading. Then came high school and football, band, dance, drama, and of course—after the discovery of the opposite sex—dating, marathon telephone calls, prom dates, Christmas parties, graduation parties. And add to the mix the emotional highs and lows of adolescence, the door slamming, the stomping around, the tears, the laughter, the conflicts, the joys.

Linda looked around her house, now so still and silent. It was hard to imagine, even now, that constant motion and clamor had once existed there—at least it had until just this morning.

Now, there was silence.

No more rock music vibrating the chandelier. (Oh, how many times she had shouted for the radio to be turned down, PLEASE!) No more friendly chatter wafting through the house, tying up the phone for hours. (What *did* they talk about for that long?)

Linda sighed, stood, and walked through the empty house, suddenly longing for the return of a little of the noise and laughter, the clamor and chaos of hands-on mothering.

But it was gone.

Forever.

Linda felt the sting of fresh tears fill her eyes.

She glanced in her bureau mirror, smiled a bit sheepishly at her reflection, then brushed away the tears.

How many times she had looked forward to finally being alone, to finally having time for herself. Yet here she was, feeling sorry for herself.

"I don't know whether to laugh or cry," she said aloud to the empty house.

Then she squinted again at her reflection, studying it intently for a few moments. There were a few more wrinkles and gray hairs than there'd been the last time she looked. Suddenly, she felt a new awareness of time's passage: The years she had given to marriage, family, and children had slipped by without a whole lot of thought about herself.

She swallowed hard and looked at herself again: Where had the young woman gone—the young woman whose youthful face once had held so many hopes and dreams? Dreams that went beyond marriage and family. Sacred dreams that she had cherished for herself alone. Where had those dreams gone?

Linda had been so many things to so many people for so long, she wondered if maybe that separate part of her inner self no longer existed, that part of her being that belonged just to her. She shuddered.

*But they're there,* she thought to herself. *I know they are. I just haven't had time to nurture them. Those dreams are someplace deep inside. And I'm going to find them.*

"Hey, kiddo," Linda said with a grin to the woman in the mirror who now grinned back at her. "It's finally time for you."

Linda liked the sound of it. She also liked the new look of steely determination in the woman's eyes. She went on, her voice growing bolder. "It's about time you discovered who you are," she said. "And it's about time you figured out what you're going to do with the rest of your life."

## Baby Boomers Hit Midlife

We are a different generation of women. Whether we've sought careers outside the home or worked creatively full time within it—we're high-energy, fast-paced, looking-to-the-twenty-first-century women.

At midlife, many of our mothers seemed to settle into a comfortable grandmotherly mode. The contrast with our grandmothers is even greater. At forty-something, they twisted their graying hair into buns and walked in thick-heeled, lace-up shoes. We, on the other hand, don a head-band over highlighted hair, pull on a fluorescent leotard, and head for the nearest fitness center. Our grandmothers cooked Sunday dinners of roast beef and mashed potatoes; we take our Sunday guests to the nearest California grill for bow-tie pesto pasta.

Though the nest has emptied, and we find ourselves alone—or nearly alone—for the first time in a couple of decades, we're of a generation that's not ready to settle back, bake cookies, and wait for the grandkids to arrive. Our high-energy, fast-paced lifestyle creates within us the need to reach for more, to stretch ourselves, to continue to grow—spiritually, emotionally, intellectually.

Thus the dilemma: We are experiencing a fresh and sad loneliness, even an awareness of our own mortality. This awareness, a symptom of midlife, carries a double whammy: We also become acutely mindful of time's passage, its *rapid*

passage. (Though we haven't yet discovered how this awareness can work *for* us. But I'm getting ahead of myself. This
good news will come later in the book.)

We may long to discover new dreams and look toward new
opportunities of growth, but the symptoms of midlife and
loneliness may fool us into believing it's too late, that in
midlife there's not enough time left to dream sacred dreams
and press on toward living out the desires of our hearts.

Guess what? I've got good news!

We may—as Linda did in the story above—find ourselves
squinting into the mirror, checking for gray hairs, and wondering what happened to the youthful face that once gazed
back at us. We may find ourselves wondering what happened
to the hopes and dreams our hearts once held. We may wonder if any of our dreams are still there, buried somewhere
deep inside.

We may, as did Linda, find ourselves wondering: Who am
I now? What will I do with the rest of my life?

The good news?

It's *not* too late to seek answers and solutions—creative,
wonderful solutions to our questions.

The time for self-discovery and dream living is now.

Today.

This moment.

And this book is only the beginning. It will take you on a
journey toward self-discovery.

We will consider our options—and explore why we will or
will not choose to dream our sacred dreams or pursue living
them. These options can fill us with trembling fear or they
can fill us with joy. They can keep us within the confines of
our "comfort zones" (more about this later too) or they can
open the door to satisfaction and excitement, to the adventure of a lifetime.

The time is now.

The choice is ours.

## We Are Living the Life of Our Choosing

Another word for option is *choice*. That brings us to our first premise: *At this moment in time we are living the life of our own choosing.*

How did we get here, living this life, be it comfortable or uncomfortable, fulfilling or unfulfilling? We didn't make one giant decision when we reached adulthood that landed us exactly where we are today. Instead, we made a series of decisions based on our given options at the time. Some choices were monumental, others were so minute, we don't remember them. Some choices were made for the good of our family. Perhaps some were made for the good of our career, or our husband's career. At times we may have felt empowered by our role in the decision-making process. Other times we may have felt that our voice counted very little. We may have sought God's will or simply hoped that he was in the boat as we set out on new seas.

This brings us back to premise number one: *Whether from a series of large or small choices, wise or ignorant choices, well-thought-out or serendipitous choices—the life we are living right now is a direct result of the choices we have made.*

## Stand Pat or Step Out

Premise number two: *All choices are based on a scale of comfort and risk.*

Do you remember in your youth when life seemed full of promise? And all the indicators used by youth told us that it would stay that way forever? Our choices were bolder. We were willing to take risks, usually without much thought of the consequences. We wanted to live life to its fullest—or at least within the parameters of what we thought "fullest" meant then. We weren't afraid to make mistakes (though we probably made plenty), take wrong turns, change our minds, or risk life and limb to try something new.

As we grew older and wiser we began to understand the consequences of our choices. We began making choices based on learned wisdom, the tried-and-true, the safe way, the (yawn) humdrum. Add to the mix a sense of responsibility for others, especially our young children, and risk-taking soon became passé.

I enrolled in a flying school when I was in my twenties. My daughter was three, and I was expecting my second child.

I made it through ground school. No problem.

I began flight instruction. No problem.

Several weeks and fifteen hours later, my instructor said, "Yup. You're ready to solo. Take 'er on up."

I taxied to the tower and let out the instructor, positioned the two-seat Cherokee on the runway, and waited for clearance for takeoff.

My palms began to sweat. My heart pounded. I could feel my knees shaking.

I was given clearance.

I turned onto the numbers, revved up the engine, and aimed for the end of the runway. My ground speed increased. At eighty-five I pulled back on the yoke and felt the exhilaration of flight as I lifted away from the ground.

I was airborne. Alone!

I had been told to stay in the pattern. That was fine with me. I kept the tower in sight as I turned downwind.

No problem.

I turned on final approach and lined up with the runway.

Oops. There was a problem.

I was too high. I cut back on the power and the plane began to drop. Too fast. The angle of descent was wrong. I knew I was in trouble. I aimed at the runway and made it to the numbers. But when I touched down the plane bounced back into the air. I pointed the nose at the earth.

It bounced into the air again, this time higher. I repeated the sequence. I could see the end of the runway coming up on me fast. But I couldn't remember how to level the plane and keep it on the ground.

I added full power and pulled back on the yoke, though the plane didn't seem to have the airspeed to climb. Miraculously, it lifted up and away from the field.

By the time I had rounded the pattern and touched down again, I had not only pounded on the door of heaven for the 7.3 minutes I was in the air, but I had also reached a conclusion I would live by for several years: My risk-taking days were over. It was time to grow up and take my responsibilities as a parent seriously.

The tried and true, the safer way, took precedence. It may have been reinforced by the two little words we often found ourselves telling our children (most of the time for good reason): "Be careful." Be cautious. Don't take chances. Whether teaching our children to look for cars before crossing a street or telling them to take care when they left for camp, above all else, we wanted our children to be safe. And we wanted to keep ourselves safe for our children. We wanted to ensure our being there for them—alive and well.

We will add another thought to premise number two: *All choices are based on a scale of comfort and risk. And most choices tip the scale more toward comfort than risk.*

It's safer. It feels better.

## Life in the Comfort Zone

Let's consider how comfort affects our choices. If given the option of choosing the tried and true or the unknown, scary, or risky—what do most people most often choose? They pick the familiar and well-worn, slipping into their choice as if into a pair of old slippers. Why? Because it feels better. Regardless of how we arrived at determining the parameters of our comfort zone, it exists within each of us. If an option we are considering lies outside that zone, the chances are greater that it will not be the option we choose.

This leads us to premise number three: *The pull of the dream must be stronger than the risk.*

I know a doctor who is in her mid-forties. A few years ago she confided in me that she really doesn't enjoy the career she chose. (This was not a whim. She has mentioned it many times.)

"What would you rather be doing?" I asked.

"I've always wanted to teach history," she said. "I went into medicine for some very wrong reasons. But now the stress is incredible. Sometimes I don't think I can make it through the day." Then she added, "Now it's too late."

"Why?" I ventured, though I already suspected the answer.

"The cut in salary alone would be impossible." She went on to lay out a host of other reasons, including her desire to pay off some property and retire early.

She never acted on her dream. Her comfort zone became her prison. She never got out. The risk was too great.

To move out of our comfort zone, the pull of the dream must be stronger than the barriers that keep us from pursuing it. There must be something about that dream that compels us to step out of the tried and true, to change our lifestyle, to risk failure, to overcome a host of obstacles (fear, guilt, unworthiness, discouragement, procrastination), in order to achieve the dream.

Another friend of mine worked as a teacher's aide in a nearby school district for ten years. Mimi is a wonderfully creative woman who enjoys children and handles them well.

One school year she worked for a teacher who had great difficulty with the class. Mimi could see the problems clearly. She could also see what needed to be done to restore order. Yet as an aide, she was powerless to act.

She said to me more than once, "I know I could teach the class better," then she would add sadly, "I just wish I had the chance."

"Then why don't you?" I asked one day. "Finish your degree. Just do it."

"Oh, no," she gasped. "I couldn't do that. Go back to school? I'm premenopausal. I'd never find my way to the admissions office, let alone find the classrooms." (Premenopausal? I hadn't heard that mentioned as an obstacle before.)

But the seed of a dream existed. My friend spent two more years in a comfort zone that became more and more intolerable. Then the desire to stretch beyond her perceived barriers became stronger. Mimi not only found the admissions office, she became a student and is well on her way to obtaining her teaching certificate.

The pull of the dream became stronger than the risk.

### Deserving to Dream

Consider premise number four: *She who is not busy being born is busy dying.* (Bob Dylan, paraphrased.)

In my early years of motherhood I remember thinking, *I can't lose sight of who I am.* I was someone's wife, someone's mother, someone's daughter, someone's daughter-in-law. The inner core got lost so easily in the busyness of raising children, nurturing the marriage, caring for extended family, and pursuing a career. There wasn't a lot of time left even to think about nurturing myself.

Hark back to those years when we had time to consider our inner self, those early years before we became so much to so many. What dream did we have that was ours alone? The question may make us feel uncomfortable. It's been a long time since we've concentrated on ourselves. It may feel selfish. It may feel self-serving. It may feel wrong.

I once discussed a dream with a friend. For months she had listened to my thinking aloud about my dream, weighing my options, hesitating to act. My friend finally said, "If one of your daughters came to you with a similar dream and asked for your help, what would you do?"

I didn't even have to think about it. I answered without hesitation, "Of course I would help her. It would be an investment in her future."

"But you don't think investing in yourself is important?"

Aha. My friend knows me very well. Or maybe she knows mothers very well. Choosing to act on our dreams—dreams that belong only to us—may be one of the most difficult but one of the most important things we ever do.

Consider who we are. Forget for a moment our human relational connections to others. Think instead about who we are in the most simple, yet most profound relationship there is: We belong to a perfect God whose every act of creation is faultless. He has made us unique and gifted. We are his dwelling place.

What kind of value does that give us? What kind of value does that give our dreams? Doesn't he want us to work toward fulfilling the potential he placed within us? Doesn't he yearn to come alongside us in the pursuit of our dream?

This may be the time that God, knowing you better than you know yourself, planned for you to stretch and grow. This time, this place, is his gift to you. Today you can take the first steps toward nurturing that most precious and intimate part of your being, to become all he would have you become. The dream you dare to dream might be the very dream he placed within you. He may have planted the seeds years ago. They may have been hidden in a secret place simply waiting to germinate and grow. Or die from lack of tending.

### Dreams + Action = The Adventure of a Lifetime

This book is about discovering dreams and, in the process, discovering more about who we are. We have reached one of the best places in life. Our years of hands-on mothering are behind us, yet we have a whole lifetime ahead. We finally have time for dream discovery. We finally have time to experience the satisfaction that comes from pursuing those dreams. We finally have time to act on those dreams.

Thus, our fifth premise: *If dreams are not followed by action, they forever remain dreams.* We've also come back to the first premise of this chapter, that the life we live is the result of the choices we make. And choosing involves action.

Dr. Robert Schuller once posed the question, "What would you attempt to do if you knew you could not fail?" Add to that Romans 8:31, "If God is for us, who can be against us?"

Wow. That opens a whole world of possibilities. It seems we have waited forever for this time to be ours. And it's finally here. Now. Just for us.

> "I believe in having a secret life with secret plans and secret dreams," says a slave mother to her daughter. "Just like having a little vegetable garden to yourself out back of your cabin like mine. You got to work it at night or real early in the morning, but it's yours. Same with dreams. Maybe you got to work them late at night or real early in the morning, but ain't nobody can take them out of your head lest they kill you, and if you work ain't nobody going to kill you, 'cause you too valuable."
>
> BARBARA CHASE-RIBOUD
> *SALLIE HEMMINGS*[1]

### Reflections

> [Your beauty] should be that of your inner self, the unfading beauty of a gentle and quiet spirit, which is of great worth in God's sight.
>
> 1 PETER 3:4

This week, celebrate the fullness that can be yours at this time in your life. Thank God for giving you this time—right here and right now—for self-discovery, for dream-discovery. Reflect on the precious and sacred dreams you once held inside (perhaps from years ago). Know that it is not too late to act on your dreams. Open your heart to explore the wonderful possibilities the future holds.

*Father, be with us on our journey. Bring to our minds those dreams that you would have us dream, those dreams that will glorify you.*

# 2

# Celebrating Solitude

*Solitude. Blessed solitude has become very important to me. I find that when I have a day alone, I just revel in it, indulge in it, bathe in it. It's the most incredible luxury.*

ELLEN BURSTYN

Solitude is finally ours. Even if we are half of a marriage partnership or have other close relationships to maintain, a new sense of "being alone" settles in when the last child leaves. We may have looked forward to this time with delight. Or we may have dreaded its coming. No matter how we feel about it, the time is here: We are women whose kids have left the nest (in some cases, with a healthy shove). We share in common a new solitude.

Some of us have filled our years of mothering with child- and family-centered activities, so when the last child leaves, our "comfort zone" is disturbed. We may find we have not looked forward to, nor are we enjoying, the "gift" of solitude that now is ours.

My friend Joy told me that after her last adult child moved out, the silence was deafening. She had been widowed six years earlier, but her children lived at home well into young adulthood, completing their degrees at a local university. During those years, Joy had made sure the door to her home was always open to her children's friends. The noise and hubbub that resulted had filled the house. Joy liked it that way.

Her younger son's marriage meant Joy was alone for the first time. Though she has a management position in a successful business, the hours she spent at home were filled with emptiness and a desperate sense of loss. The last thing Joy wanted was the "gift" of solitude.

Some of us, however, accept our new status with gratitude. We tolerated the chatter of excited teens while trying to watch *Masterpiece Theater,* or the screams (we suspected weren't fatal) for "Mom!" from the backyard while reading the last pages of a great mystery. We looked forward with delight to the day when solitude would finally be ours. And now that it's here, we can finish the latest Sue Grafton, or relax with a cup of English tea and all three movements of Beethoven's *Emperor Concerto*—alone.

Another friend, Connie, began planning months ahead for the September her daughter would leave for college. Her husband, Michael, who worked for an international import- export company, traveled frequently. Her son had moved out two years earlier.

Connie, energetic and creative, had put her all into motherhood, even choosing to stay at home while her children were growing up. Through the years she volunteered in the children's classrooms, participated in PTA and, at one point, ran for an opening on the local school board (though she was not elected).

When her son, Brett, made first chair trumpet in his high school marching band, Connie was delighted (she had played flute in the concert band during her own high school years). During Brett's second year in band, the director announced plans for the students to travel to Australia—provided they could raise the funds. Connie, of course, volunteered to head up the fund-raising activities. And she did it successfully.

Her daughter, Karen, was a top student, excelling in history and government classes. Each of Karen's three years in high school she tried out for and made the U.S. Constitution team. When Karen's team made the national finals and traveled to Washington, D.C., Connie and her husband volunteered to help coach the students as well as travel with them as volunteer chaperones.

Connie planned to fill her coming days of solitude with the same care with which she had filled her days of motherhood. She listed all the things she had wanted to do but hadn't had time to do. She loved her children, cherished the memories of her childrearing days, but looked forward to the life ahead.

I asked her why.

"I'm going to celebrate the day I finally have time alone." She went on to tell me that she wanted to replenish her emotional energy through simply soaking up those things around her she hadn't had time for in years: music, books, nature's beauty—alone. "I want to work with Michael on our relationship as well," she added. "It will be the first time that we've been alone in years. But first I need to find the part of me that's been lost while I cared for everyone else." She was quiet a moment. "Through the years I felt I might not have the chance to get in touch with 'me' again. Now I've finally got the time."

Though Joy and Connie view differently the years that stretch ahead in this new life phase, they share with us a common thread: A new solitude is ours—to celebrate or to mourn.

## Seeing the Elephant

You're probably wondering what an elephant has to do with the steps we're taking toward following our dreams. Stay with me—there is a connection. I promise.

During this time in our lives we are moving out of the known—busy lives filled with the time and energy of raising children—into the unknown—lives filled with extra time for quiet reflection. We may feel uneasy, uncomfortable, perhaps downright fearful.

This is a good time to ask ourselves, how comfortable *are* we with being alone? Maybe it is better asked: How comfortable are we with ourselves? Think about it: We have spent a lifetime being someone's daughter, wife, mother, daughter-in-law, boss, employee. The list goes on. If we picture the whole of us as a pie chart, each of the slices has to do with relationships. They are based on time spent with another person or persons.

What about that part of ourselves that doesn't appear on a chart—the core of who we are, that invisible and most intimate part of our being? As with most mothers and career persons in the twentieth century, we probably haven't had much time to get to know that part of ourselves.

Now we finally have the time.

And the solitude.

Oh, dear.

That may be the last thing we want to do.

Back to the elephant.

During the westward migration of the nineteenth century, many emigrants left homes in the East that had been surrounded by forests and lush green terrain. They were used to mountains and rolling hills, vegetation, and, in many cases, towns filled with people. They had never been in open spaces without a canopy of trees overhead. When their wagon trains pulled onto the Great Plains under a sky that stretched endlessly before them, they saw a bleak and arid land, flat and treeless, disappearing into a horizon miles in the distance. The phrase "seeing the elephant," which originated from first-time circusgoers' awe at the immensity of the show's elephant, was commonly used slang among the pioneers to describe the awesome perils, seen and imagined, that plagued many travelers and left more than a few feeling overwhelmed. Some looked at the never-ending miles stretching out before them, declared they had "seen the elephant," and turned back. They could not bear the fear induced by the strange, vast terrain.

One woman's journal records her feelings of dismay and anxiety as she imagined herself shrinking to the point of nothingness. Many others (both men and women) recorded feeling various degrees of discomfort. One traveler related: "The first experience of the plains, like the first sail with a 'cap' full of wind, is apt to be sickening" (Richard Irving Dodge, *The Plains of the Great West*). "Loneliness, thy other name, thy one true synonym, is prairie," wrote William A. Quayle in *The Prairie and the Sea* (1905).

Most of us don't have a problem with wide open spaces. Mental health professionals tell us, however, that preexisting "free-floating anxiety" can settle into specific thoughts of discomfort ("something bad is going to happen to me") when we step into situations where there is no familiar frame of reference.

When we find ourselves alone, after all the years we've been an integral part of our children's lives, we no longer have that "frame of reference" that has defined an enormous part of our lives. Even if we are fulfilled in our marriages and careers, there can still be a place within us that seems as empty and spacious as the Great Plains seemed to the early pioneers.

We may have held anxieties at bay through frantically busy days spread throughout our lifetime. Now they can take on exaggerated proportions that seem larger than life. This is what had happened to my friend Joy. Widowed early, she had been left completely alone when her young adult children (and their friends) moved out. Suddenly she was forced to face anxieties she had kept from her consciousness since her husband's death years earlier.

"I hadn't realized how powerless I felt," Joy told me. "I had no choice in my husband's dying, no choice in my children's leaving, and no choice in having to live alone." Then she added sadly, "I didn't have control over any of those events. I think it was that sense of powerlessness that caused me the most anxiety. I know now it wasn't realistic—but I began to think that all circumstances controlled me. I was a victim. No matter what I did, I couldn't change those circumstances."

"Then what *did* change?" I asked. I had noticed that she now seemed more at peace with herself than she had in months.

"I finally realized that I do have control over that inner part of myself. I can choose how I want to live my life. And that makes a big difference in how I feel about being alone." Then she smiled and added, "The funny thing is—I didn't discover any of this until I *was* alone. It's ironic that being alone was the last thing I wanted."

### God Is with Us in Our Loneliness

In our loneliness, it may help to remember that our pain is part of being loved—by our families, by God. It's life's most painful experiences that cause us to grow, that bring us into our fullness—that make us real.

I am reminded of the well-known story *The Velveteen Rabbit* by Margery Williams.

*"What is REAL?" asked the Rabbit one day, when they were lying side by side near the nursery fender, before Nana came to tidy the room. "Does it mean having things that buzz inside you and a stick-out handle?"*

(We may think that there's a "quick fix"—something attractive we can do externally that will cure our loneliness.)

*"Real isn't how you are made," said the Skin Horse. "It's a thing that happens to you. When a child loves you for a long, long time, not just to play with, but REALLY loves you, then you become Real."*

(We mothers, of all people, know what that feels like!)

*"Does it hurt?" asked the Rabbit.*

(The hurt of our loneliness is all the more profound because of that REAL love that we have for our children and because of our separation from them.)

*"Sometimes," said the Skin Horse, for he was always truthful. "When you are Real you don't mind being hurt."*

(This, too, is true!)

*"Does it happen all at once, like being wound up," he asked, "or bit by bit?"*

(The healing from the hurt of our loneliness also takes time.)

*"It doesn't happen all at once," said the Skin Horse. "You become. It takes a long time. That's why it doesn't often happen to people who break easily, or have sharp edges, or who have to be carefully kept. Generally, by the time you are Real, most of your hair has been loved off, and your eyes drop out and you get loose in the joints and very shabby. But these things don't matter at all, because once you are Real you can't be ugly, except to people who don't understand."*[1]

How many of us feel just like the Skin Horse? What a vivid description of motherhood! All those years of loving and being loved have caused our hair to be loved off and our eyes to have dropped out and our joints to be loose and us to feel shabby.

But the good news is that women who have gone through two decades of childrearing don't break easily. And in the fresh pain of our loneliness God is still working with us, helping us "become" who he would have us be, helping us become real.

## Springs of Water in Desert Places

Whether we rejoice or tremble at the thought of becoming real, we may still be feeling lonely in our new solitude and find it difficult to think that this stage of our life is a positive thing. We may feel abandoned by our children (even though we *know* better) or by God.

Tim Hansel, in *Through the Wilderness of Loneliness*, writes:

> Loneliness is not a time of abandonment . . . it just feels that way. It's actually a time of encounter at new levels with the only One who can fill that empty place in our hearts.
> Loneliness need not be an enemy . . . it can be a friend.
> Loneliness need not be an interruption in our lives . . . it can be a gift.
> Loneliness need not be an obstacle . . . it can be an invitation.
> Loneliness need not be a problem . . . it can be an opportunity.
> Loneliness need not be a dead end . . . it can be an adventure![2]

Someone once said, "Like it or not, we are as vulnerable to loneliness as we are to the common cold." Women who have spent decades with lives intricately intertwined with children and family are probably even more vulnerable. We may "catch" loneliness more readily than the common cold. But the pain we feel is more akin to double pneumonia.

Loneliness, however, can be a gift. It can be used as a time to quiet ourselves before God, to allow him to teach us about who we are in this stage of our lives. Elisabeth Elliot said, "The pain of loneliness is one way in which [God] gets our attention." Tim Hansel says that loneliness "is a gift that opens up our heart to yearn for His peace. It is a longing for a deeper experience of His presence." He also writes that loneliness "can be an unexpected invitation to discover God's love and mercy at a previously unexplored level."

We may still feel we would prefer turning back the clock, returning to the "comfort zone" of our earlier years, if only we could. But what if this place of solitude is the very place we need to be before beginning our journey of self-discovery? What if this place is where we will find a hidden freshwater spring, a spring we never before knew existed? We may find around us a landscape that we once considered bleak taking on a beauty we hadn't seen before—a precious place of beauty we would have missed if it hadn't been for this new time in our lives.

God tells us in Isaiah 41:18:

> I will make rivers flow on barren heights,
>     and springs within the valleys.
> I will turn the desert into pools of water,
>     and the parched ground into springs.

We are about to embark on a pilgrimage of self-discovery. What better way to begin than in that place of solitude where we can meet God. "God speaks in the silence of the heart. And we listen" (Mother Teresa). This brings us to the premise: *Before we can dream we must know ourselves. To know ourselves we must spend time alone with God.*

Take a few minutes to read Psalm 84:1–5.

In verses 1–2, we may picture the "dwelling place" or the "courts of the LORD" as a heavenly realm that exists beyond the tangible clay of our earth. However, I like to think of this "dwelling place" as an inner place of quiet where we can commune with the One who knows us and loves us best. This is the place where we can get to know him better and discover who we are in him.

Our place of solitude is a sacred place, containing the most intimate part of our being. It is also a place where we find springs of refreshment for the journey ahead. It is here we meet God, the Friend who will be with us as we "set our hearts on pilgrimage." Here we find who we are before him. In our solitude, the external distractions of people and events fall away. We can return again and again to commune with him, to worship and adore him, to think about who he is.

In the prologue I mentioned that this book is one of active interaction, that you would be keeping a personal record of your journey. If you haven't already, please take out your journal and write in it the above passage from Psalm 84. Underline verse 4: "Blessed are those who dwell in your house; they are ever praising you."

If we are to be ever praising God, our first step may be to think about who he says he is. In your journal, write, "This is who my Friend is," then record (from the following headings and verses) those verses that speak especially to you:

He is accessible: "The LORD is near to all who call on him" (Ps. 145:18).

He is faithful: "I am with you and will watch over you wherever you go. . . . I will not leave you until I have done what I have promised you" (Gen. 28:15).

"I will lead the blind by ways they have not known, along unfamiliar paths I will guide them; I will turn the darkness into light before them and make the rough places smooth. These are the things I will do; I will not forsake them" (Isa. 42:16).

He is our guide: "Since you are my rock and my fortress, for the sake of your name lead and guide me" (Ps. 31:3).

"I will instruct you and teach you in the way you should go; I will counsel you and watch over you" (Ps. 32:8).

"If I rise on the wings of the dawn, if I settle on the far side of the sea, even there your hand will guide me, your right hand will hold me fast" (Ps. 139:9–10).

He knows us: "O LORD, you have searched me and you know me. You know when I sit and when I rise; you perceive my thoughts from afar. You discern my going out and my lying down; you are familiar with all my ways. Before a word is on my tongue you know it completely, O LORD" (Ps. 139:1–4).

He is love: "You are precious and honored in my sight, and . . . I love you" (Isa. 43:4).

He is merciful: "The LORD your God is gracious and compassionate. He will not turn his face from you" (2 Chron. 30:9).

He is ever present: "Surely the LORD is in this place, and I was not aware of it" (Gen. 28:16).

He is our preserver: "The LORD's unfailing love surrounds the man who trusts in him" (Ps. 32:10).

Think of it. This is the God who is with us on our pilgrimage!

### Giants in the Land

We may ask ourselves: *If I belong to such a God as this, what can go wrong?* Remember the elephants? We've taken care of those. But now there may be giants in the land. And one of them may be an inaccurate view of God and who we are in relation to him.

How we see God can be distorted by experiences, particularly during early childhood. For instance, if we had a negative relationship with our father, our view of God, the Father, can be clouded. An authoritarian or rigid upbringing can give us a false idea of God, the Judge. We may not be able to understand a God of justice and mercy. If parents or others involved in our upbringing were uninterested or indifferent, we may have difficulty believing in a God who is intensely interested and personally involved in our lives.

When we have trouble with a "heart understanding" of God, it may help to remember the difficulties of the Israelites on their journey to Canaan. It is a story that reminds us how easy it is to forget that God is who he says he is. We, like the Israelites, can get entangled in our own misperceptions, our own distortions, and those of others. Sometimes we, as they did, forget the evidence of God's interaction with us, the tangible evidence of his blessings. We may have difficulty believing his promises.

You may remember the miracles God performed when he led the Israelites out of slavery in Egypt. His presence had been with them in a mighty way: He had parted the Red Sea and destroyed their enemies; he had provided manna and quail and turned bitter water to sweet to provide for them physically; he had gone before them as a pillar of cloud by day and a pillar of fire by night.

They were within 250 miles of the Promised Land when an astounding thing happened. They forgot who their God was.

Moses, following God's directive, had sent twelve spies into Canaan to check out the lay of the land. After forty days, they returned. It was one of those good news/bad news stories. First the good news. It took two spies to carry (on a pole between them) a branch bearing a single cluster of grapes. Others carried baskets heaped with pomegranates and figs. When Moses asked about the land, they said: "We went into the land to which you sent us, and it does flow with milk and honey!" (Num. 13:27). This was *tangible* evidence of the truth of God's promise to them.

Then the spies added the bad news: "But the people who live there are powerful, and the cities are fortified and very large" (v. 28). Within a few lines of dialogue, the evidence of God's promise and protection was overlooked—forgotten as if it had never existed.

Then Caleb (one of the two sensible spies among them) stated boldly, "We should go up and take possession of the land, for we can certainly do it" (v. 30).

No one listened.

"We can't attack those people; they are stronger than we are," moaned the spies who had gone with him (v. 31). Then the bad news got worse. Rumors began to spread like wildfire. "The land we explored devours those living in it. All the people we saw there are of great size," they said (v. 32). But that wasn't enough. Distortions based on fear took over. "We seemed like grasshoppers in our own eyes, and we looked the same to them" (v. 33).

Numbers 14 tells us that night all the people wept and grumbled. "If only we had died in Egypt! Or in the desert! Why is the LORD bringing us to this land only to let us fall by the sword? Our wives and children will be taken as plunder" (vv. 2–3). Talk about spiraling downward! Then they asked, "Wouldn't it be better for us to go back to Egypt?"

It didn't matter that God had performed miracle after miracle to release them from bondage in Egypt and care for them on their journey to the land he clearly had promised them.

God hadn't changed—but their view of him had. They had been blinded to his sovereignty and providential care. The only thing they had left was fear.

This may seem extreme, but it is a reminder of the distortions we may face.

Ellie, for example, is a woman I know who thought she had a clear picture of God. It wasn't until she finally had time to spend in her "quiet place," alone with him, that she realized something vital was missing in the relationship. It hadn't occurred to her before, but planning moments of solitude to meet God in this way wasn't something she wanted to do. She recognized that though she had been busy raising children and pursuing a career, for years she had avoided pursuing an intimate time with God.

"Why do I feel so uncomfortable with this?" Ellie had telephoned to discuss her dilemma. "I should be looking forward to this quiet time with God. I feel guilty that I don't."

"Do you think God is looking forward to meeting you?" I asked.

There was a moment of thoughtful silence. "Well, no," she said. "I guess I feel he doesn't really care if I'm there or not. The burden is on me—you know, something I feel I *need* to do."

"As in *have* to do," I said gently, then went on. "You feel God doesn't care whether you're there or not. And you feel this meeting is something you're required to do. No wonder you're avoiding it."

We began exploring Ellie's spiritual history, searching for clues in her past that would help us understand her present feelings. She began to talk about her early memories of growing up in the church.

"My family was always more concerned with doing than being. That seemed to be the only way to measure up to God's standards," she said.

"God's standards?"

"Well, I guess they were standards set by the church, the denomination, actually. But the way they were presented made me feel they were straight from God." Ellie's voice sounded as though something inside still believed in the standards she remembered from many years ago. Ellie went on to describe the list of do's and don'ts.

"You haven't mentioned anything about God's grace and love," I said. "Were these taught at all?"

"I don't remember it," Ellie said. "If love and grace were there, they didn't receive the attention 'God, the Judge' got." She sighed. "Everything seemed to focus on the external—not the internal."

"How did that feel to you as a child?"

"It was a simple translation—if I *did* right, I would be loved. If I *did* wrong, I wouldn't be."

"By your parents?"

Ellie was quiet a moment before she answered. "Yes. But also by God."

"Do you still feel you have to please God by doing the right thing to gain his love?"

"If I'm honest—yes."

Ellie then went on to tell of her father, an opinionated man, who believed in a God of black-and-white values. If you lived right, God smiled on you. If not? Well, who knows what could happen? It was never really defined. But to a sensitive child with a vivid imagination, that "who knows" became something she didn't want to find out.

Ellie said her mother was equally concerned with doing the right thing. She never raised her voice when Ellie misbehaved. She simply stopped speaking to her daughter, sometimes for hours, even days. Ellie's mother was also a woman who, because of the standards of the church community, was obsessed with "what others would think." The true measure of right and wrong was never clear to the young Ellie.

Ellie related that after she became an adult, she looked back at her childhood and saw many of the admonitions as they actually were: man-made rules. As the years passed, she felt she had grown beyond the rigid views of her parents. She held it all at a distance, not realizing that as she did so, she also held God at a distance.

As we talked, Ellie told me of her divorce several years earlier and its impact on her spiritual life. She still struggled with feelings of guilt and rejection.

"I know that the divorce was the only healthy thing I could do for myself and for my sons," she said. "For years I tried to make the marriage work. My husband was an alcoholic. I couldn't tolerate the abuse any longer."

"But you feel the judgment of others—and of God?" I asked.

"Oh, yes. It's not something I consciously think about, but deep inside it's always with me," Ellie said.

"Your father wasn't sure how God might punish you if you stepped out of the realm of 'right and wrong.' Your mother wouldn't speak to you if you 'misbehaved.' Now you, having already judged yourself, try to have quiet time with a God who, in your mind, is harsh, silent, and indifferent."

Neither one of us said anything for a moment. Then I added quietly, "I wouldn't want time alone with a God like that either."

Talk about giants. Talk about false reports by well-meaning spies!

Several weeks passed before I talked with Ellie again. When she called, her voice reflected a dramatic change. "Once I understood why I was so uncomfortable being alone with God, it helped," she said. "There is still a lot of unraveling to do, but I'm beginning to see what I was doing."

"What do you mean?" I asked.

"I have been projecting my negative self-judgment onto God. Without really thinking about it, I had assumed the judgment was correct. I can't tell you the relief I felt when I discovered I was wrong. At one point—after I read the verses you gave me about who God says he is—a surprising thought hit me."

"What was that?"

Ellie laughed. "I thought about how arrogant I was for believing that what I did or didn't do could change who God is." She was quiet a moment, then added, "I know it's much more complicated than this, but I like to believe that God is bigger than all that—that he's much bigger than my concept of him."

There are more of us "Ellies" in the world than we know. We have been blinded, much as the Israelites outside the Promised Land were blinded, to who our God really is. Our circumstances may be different, but God's truth and his promises have been distorted by well-meaning "spies" who have given us an inaccurate picture of the Promised Land and the God who is leading us there.

As with Ellie, we may have gotten the message that we must earn God's love. Yet we forever fall short of the mark. What can we do?

## Knowing and Being Known

If we are trying to deserve God's love, we can *do* nothing. No matter what we *do*, we can never deserve his love, *period*. Where does that leave us? I've got wonderful news: It leaves us in the best possible place.

God's love for us is based on his knowledge of us, knowledge having to do with his sovereignty and grace. It is he who takes the initiative in loving, choosing, redeeming, calling, guiding, and preserving; not because we earn his favor, but because he is who he is and cannot be otherwise.

When we think about who God says he is, as in the verses recorded earlier in this chapter, we realize that God, in full knowledge of us—the best about us, the worst about us— pours into us more love and compassion than we could ever deserve. J. I. Packer, in *Knowing God,* puts it this way:

> There is tremendous relief in knowing that His love to me is utterly realistic, based at every point on prior knowledge of the worst about me, so that no discovery now can disillusion Him about me, in the way I am so often disillusioned about myself, and quench His determination to bless me. There is, certainly, great cause for humility in the thought that He sees all the twisted things about me that my fellow-men do not see (and am I glad!), and that He sees more corruption in me than that which I see in myself (which, in all conscience, is enough). There is, however, equally great incentive to worship and love God in the thought that, for some unfathomable reason, He wants me as His friend, and desires to be my friend.[3]

## He Is *For* Us

When David considered how perfectly he was known by God, he said, "Such knowledge is too wonderful for me" (Ps. 139:6). And we can add to that, as did David, in verse 17, "How precious to me are your thoughts, O God!"

In light of (or shall we say, in *spite* of) God's knowledge of us, let's look at how he feels about us. In your journal, write, "God has said this about me." Then write the following verses, substituting your name where appropriate.

As an example, in writing Isaiah 43:4, you would write, "(your name) is precious and honored in my sight and . . . I love (her)." Continue with the following verses, taking time to reflect on your value in God's eyes.

"I have summoned you by name; you are mine" (Isa. 43:1).

"I have loved you with an everlasting love; I have drawn you with loving-kindness" (Jer. 31:3).

"The LORD your God is with you, he is mighty to save. He will take great delight in you, he will quiet you with his love, he will rejoice over you with singing" (Zeph. 3:17).

"I have engraved you on the palms of my hands; your walls are ever before me" (Isa. 49:16).

"For the LORD takes delight in his people; he crowns the humble with salvation" (Ps. 149:4).

"O LORD, you have searched me and you know me. . . . I praise you because I am fearfully and wonderfully made" (Ps. 139:1, 14).

"He who loves me will be loved by my Father, and I too will love him and show myself to him" (John 14:21).

"For whoever touches you touches the apple of his eye" (Zech. 2:8).

## It's Time to Celebrate!

This is the God who knows us, loves us, and is *for* us as we prepare for our journey of self-discovery. We are wonderfully made, the products of his artistry and creativity. We are women created by a God who does nothing halfway. He is pleased with who he has made us to be: He rejoices over us with singing!

He is our Advocate as we begin this quest to "enlarge the place of our tents and stretch our tent curtains wide."

He is our Protector when we meet any real or imagined "giants in the land." (An unclear picture of God is just one of those giants. We may meet others along the way: giants of discouragement, anger, fear, guilt, unworthiness, those that tell us we don't deserve to do what we're doing, pursue what we're pursuing, dream what we're dreaming. But more about these later.)

He is our Deliverer. When we meet these giants, we won't be alone. He says to us: "You will not have to fight this battle. Take up your positions; stand firm and see the deliverance the LORD will give you. . . . Do not be afraid; do not be discouraged. Go out to face them tomorrow, and the LORD will be with you" (2 Chron. 20:17).

He is a Friend who will go with us on our journey.

We meet him in our solitude.

He speaks to us in the silence of our hearts.

And we listen.

<center>~~~</center>

## Reflections

The LORD said, "Go out and stand on the mountain in the presence of the LORD, for the LORD is about to pass by." Then a great and powerful wind tore the mountains apart and shattered the rocks before the LORD, but the LORD was not in the wind. After the wind there was an earthquake, but the LORD was not in the earthquake. After the earthquake came a fire, but the LORD was not in the fire. And after the fire came a gentle whisper.

1 KINGS 19:11–12

This week, listen for the Lord's gentle whisper. Rejoice in the solitude that allows you to hear him speak. Celebrate your intimacy with him in the quiet, still silence of your heart. Lift your voice in praise: You are spending time with the almighty God and Creator of the universe!

*Dear Lord, help us find that quiet place inside where we can hear your voice. Draw us away from those things that would distract us. Let us know you better!*

# 3

# It's Okay to Love Ourselves

*If we feel ourselves valuable, then we will feel our time to be valuable, and if we feel our time to be valuable, then we will want to use it well.*

M. SCOTT PECK
*THE ROAD LESS
TRAVELED*

## Self-Love: The Good, the Bad, and the Ugly

Understanding our worth is the cornerstone of self-discipline. If we feel valuable, we are more likely to care for ourselves emotionally, physically, and spiritually. Self-caring is okay if our worth is based on our Creator's image in us.

### The Good: We're Made in His Image

*It is the morning of the sixth day. A newborn sun casts its pure light across the earth's sky.*

*A song begins. At first it's faint, heard only by animals, small and large, who leave their nests and hollows and look heavenward toward the sound. The music rises joyfully with the wind, kissing the meadowlands, its tone holding more power, beauty, and compassion as it builds.*

*The music cradles the young earth: First and most powerful, the loving voice of the Creator as he sings creation's song. Then, from the deep heavens, he is joined by the morning stars as they lift their praise songs to their King. And from across the universe, an echo of joy from a choir of angels. On the lush and verdant newborn earth, a lone man sleeps.*

*Suddenly, the song becomes softer, shaded with tenderness. The King kneels beside the man and takes from him bone and sinew. With love and reverence, he carefully forms the being who becomes his final act of creation: the being he calls Woman.*

*The woman stirs slightly, then opens her eyes. Curious wonder lights her face as she turns to watch a butterfly dancing across the meadow grasses. Then her gaze moves to the leafy branches above where she lies. A dogwood blossom peeks from beneath the foliage. Laughing in delight, she stands and touches her nose to its fragrant petals, then carefully inspects its delicate beauty.*

*A movement in a nearby thicket catches her attention. A deer with a regal crown of antlers moves toward her, and she runs across the mossy ground to greet him, first touching the cool leather of his nose, then stroking the sun-warmed fur on his neck.*

*Then the woman hears a voice speak her name. She turns, a look of joyful expectancy. The voice is that of her Creator. Her God!*

Eve. The mother of humanity (Gen. 3:20). Created in beauty and splendor. Formed with intricate complexity. The final touch of creation.

What a wonder to consider her creation. What a wonder to consider our own!

God rejoiced at Eve's creation, taking joy in the woman he made *and* in her daughters who would follow centuries later. Our blueprint had been completed; our value was established. Job 38:7 tells us that when God laid the foundation of the earth "the morning stars sang together and all the angels shouted for joy." Consider that these angelic beings were singing praise to the Creator for his mighty works, reflecting his deep pleasure in his creation (Gen. 1:31)—from the expanse of the universe to the human bodies of Adam and Eve.

Zephaniah 3:17 emphasizes God's delight in us: "He will take great delight in you, he will quiet you with his love, he will rejoice over you with singing." Can you imagine that your Creator delights in you—his creation—so much that he rejoices over you with singing? That he considers your very existence worthy of his undivided attention, that there is never a moment you are out of his thoughts, that your name is engraved on the palms of his hands (Isa. 49:16)? What value we hold in his eyes!

Let's think for a moment about the miracle of who we are.

James D. Watson, one of the discoverers of DNA, says in *The Double Helix* that he knew he had come upon the right DNA structure when he saw that it looked "pretty." And he's right. The spiral double helix chromosomes—holding the entire design for a human being—look like colorful, dancing ladders. Graceful. Fearfully and wonderfully, *beautifully*, made (Ps. 139:14). Isn't that just like our God?

And the nuclei in each of our body's cells contains the same blueprint. It's astounding to think that there is enough tightly coiled DNA in one body's cells' nuclei to reach the moon and return 20,000 times if it were laid out in a line!

Each of us developed from a single fertilized egg cell. That one cell developed into trillions of cells that carry out all the functions of our body. Scientists haven't yet discovered how the developing cells of this tiny, growing embryo know how to organize themselves into separate organs and body parts. Think about it: How does each cell know whether it's going to be a strand of hair or a toenail?

Think for a moment about your own design. If you were born in the United States, the day of your birth probably was shared with some 15,000 other babies. Some 3 million were born the same year, yet not one was the same as another (except in the case of identical twins).

You are the genetic combination of one of about 400 of your mother's egg cells with one of 360 million sperm cells. You might have been any one of about 144 billion distinct human beings coming from your parents alone! Yet God's touch and perfect timing determined exactly who and what you would be.

You will grow at a remarkable rate. In only 17 days you will begin to form blood cells, by 18 days, a heart, and by day 20, the foundation for a brain, spinal cord, and nervous system.

This nervous system will eventually be the most efficient in the world for message transmission; each nerve fiber will carry messages at a speed of 150 yards per second—or 300 miles an hour. The system will eventually contain more than 10 billion nerve cells forming interconnections through your body. Each nerve cell is cross-connected to 1,000 others—a total of 10 trillion connections!

Twelve million nerve endings will form your nose, which will later enjoy the fragrance of a rose or the aroma of fresh-baked bread. One hundred thousand nerve cells will be devoted to reacting to sounds—the ticking of a grandfather clock, the piccolo in *Stars and Stripes Forever*. The piano has only 240 strings, but each of your ears will have more than 15,000 hair cells in the cochlea to detect the smallest variations in sound.

By the end of your first month you will have grown from one cell to billions of cells, from a tiny bit of protoplasm to intricately organized groups of cells that will make up your nervous, muscular, circulatory, digestive, and skeletal systems. And you are still only one-quarter of an inch in length.

By eight weeks your fingers and toes are formed. Your heart begins to beat. By month three you are kicking your feet and curling your toes. Your hand forms a fist. A few weeks later, your heart is strong enough to pump about 25 quarts of blood through your body each day. Eventually, this heart will pump more than 72,000 quarts of blood through more than 100,000 miles of vessels in a 24-hour day. It will beat more than 100,000 times each day and will continue to do so for up to 70, 80, maybe 90 years.

You have had cartilage throughout your body from about the second month. During the sixth month it begins to be replaced by bone. You will eventually have 222 bones to support all the soft body parts. And these bones will be strong! For example, your shin bone (which seems so fragile) will be able to sustain a weight of two tons!

Consider the loving design and construction of your body from the moment of your conception through birth . . . and beyond, from one cell through the complexity of the adult, female body. Every part of your being was carefully planned and implemented according to your Creator's perfect plan.

You are not a serendipitous whim of nature. You are a carefully orchestrated masterpiece, created, composed, with beauty and dignity and complexity by the Master Musician, our Lord, our Creator.

We are different from all others in his Creation: We humans are created in God's image, that is, with the capacity to share a portion of his nature, his holiness, his goodness, his compassion, his righteousness.

We consider the wonder of our exterior being. But it is nothing compared to the miracle inside. The apostle Paul tells us in 2 Corinthians 4:7 that our bodies as fashioned by God hold a glorious treasure—the power of his spirit living in us! With David in Psalm 8:3–5 we can say,

When I consider your heavens,
　　the work of your fingers,
the moon and the stars,
　　which you have set in place,
what is man that you are mindful of him,
　　the son of man that you care for him?
You made him a little lower than the heavenly beings
　　and crowned him with glory and honor.

### *His* Female *Creation*

We are not just valued as one-half of mankind, but we are valued also *because* we are that female half. Our very femininity is compared to that part of God's being that is nurturing, compassionate, creative (in the purest sense).

From Eve's first breath of life through the generations to Mary, Jesus' mother, down through the centuries to you and me, it is woman whom God chose to give birth—to join him in the act of creation. (Not that men don't play an important role!) But it is only woman who knows the indescribable and deep-pained joy of bringing forth a child from her own body.

In one of the most tender passages in Isaiah, God compares his bond with Israel to that of a mother with an infant:

> For you will nurse and be satisfied
> 　　at her comforting breasts;
> you will drink deeply
> 　　and delight in her overflowing abundance. . . .
> you will nurse and be carried on her arm
> 　　and dandled on her knees.
> As a mother comforts her child,
> 　　so will I comfort you.
>
> ISAIAH 66:11–13

God chose to use the metaphor of the bride (again a female-only role) as his beloved Israel (in the Old Testament) and as the church (in the New Testament). He is the Bridegroom, filled with deep compassion toward his bride.

Take out your journal. Consider these verses and write those words, phrases, or entire verses that speak to you of God's compassion toward *you*.

"For your Maker is your husband—
   the LORD Almighty is his name—
the Holy One of Israel is your Redeemer;
   he is called the God of all the earth.
The LORD will call you back
   as if you were a wife deserted and distressed in spirit—
a wife who married young,
   only to be rejected," says your God.
"For a brief moment I abandoned you,
   but with deep compassion I will bring you back.
In a surge of anger
   I hid my face from you for a moment,
but with everlasting kindness
   I will have compassion on you,"
says the LORD your Redeemer.

ISAIAH 54:5–8

God's tender, unconditional love toward his "bride" provides the foundation for his covenant relationship with his people.

In the following verse, the bridegroom's covenant with his bride is symbolic of God's covenant with a murderously disobedient Israel. Yet he says of his beloved:

I will betroth you to me forever;
   I will betroth you in righteousness and justice,
   in love and compassion.
I will betroth you in faithfulness,
   and you will acknowledge the LORD.

HOSEA 2:19

And in Revelation, the imagery of the wedding speaks of Christ's compassion for the church, his bride, for those who love him and for whom he will someday come and gather to himself in a mighty cloud of glory:

> Hallelujah!
> For our LORD God Almighty reigns.
> Let us rejoice and be glad
> and give him glory!
> For the wedding of the Lamb has come,
> and his bride has made herself ready.
>
> REVELATION 19:6–7

### *His* Unique *Creation*

We are familiar with Psalm 139, though I must admit I became most intimately aware of it when I was pregnant with my older daughter, Melinda. So when I read it through the years, I thought most often of how it related to my daughters, not to me. But let's take a look at a few verses again, this time thinking about ourselves as we read:

> For you created my inmost being;
> you knit me together in my mother's womb. . . .
> My frame was not hidden from you
> when I was made in the secret place.
> When I was woven together in the depths of the earth,
> your eyes saw my unformed body.
> All the days ordained for me
> were written in your book
> before one of them came to be.
>
> PSALM 139:13, 15–16

Oh, how our God must love us! He created us, and most of us have considered and accepted his creation as part of who we are. But his effort toward our creation didn't just stop there! Psalm 139:1–3 tells us that he knows us more intimately than we know ourselves:

> O LORD, you have searched me
> and you know me.

You know when I sit and when I rise;
   you perceive my thoughts from afar.
You discern my going out and my lying down;
   you are familiar with all my ways.

God has been acutely aware of everything about us from the moment of our first cell division through each second, minute, hour, decade of our years, from childhood and young adulthood through marriage and motherhood and into our middle years. He has been there, with us, gently watching, ever caring, guiding (though sometimes harshly, we might think), but constantly aware of us, coming alongside us on our life's journey.

He is with you this moment, as intimately aware of you as he was when he formed you in the "secret place."

Talk about intimacy! Talk about his love toward us!

Think of it! God's imagery of his beloved—that in which he chose to portray his most deeply intimate and most profound love toward all mankind—is feminine. A woman. His bride. With the psalmist, our hearts soar in praise:

How precious to me are your thoughts, O God!
   How vast is the sum of them!
Were I to count them,
   they would outnumber the grains of sand.

PSALM 139:17–18

Please take out your journal and reread the thoughts you recorded in chapter two—those relating to God's love for you. Take a few minutes to dwell on your value as his unique creation.

Make a list of those things about yourself that are unique. Think about how each of these brings glory to your Creator as you reflect to others around you who he is (in the way only *you* can). Thank him for each of these characteristics.

Celebrate your uniqueness! Don't be afraid to be glad for who you are—who God made you to be. Think of it! Each of your cells, whether plump or thin, each bone, whether long or short, each of your genes, whether artistic or pragmatic, is his creation. They are stacked together in just the way that makes you uniquely you. You are one of a kind! You are as unique as your fingerprints.

I think about the Bill and Gloria Gaither song that I sang with my daughters when they were preschoolers. The first two lines went something like this:

> I am a Promise;
> I am a Possibility[1]

How I smiled and hugged my little girls as we sang, willing them to feel good about themselves, to feel happy and glad about who they were, to celebrate their promise (their value) and their potential (all they could become).

Yet how comfortable can I be singing such a song—or even daring to whisper such words—to *myself*?

Gulp.

I have to admit, that's not comfortable at all.

How about you?

Maybe we need to explore this further.

### *The Bad: We Must Love Ourselves*

Consider for a moment Christ's words to the Pharisees in Matthew 22:37–39: "'Love the Lord your God with all your heart and with all your soul and with all your mind.' This is the first and greatest commandment. And the second is like it: 'Love your neighbor as yourself.'"

I know. You're wondering how can this be bad? After all, these commandments, in Jesus' own words, are the two greatest, most important, all-encompassing commandments in Scripture.

There is nothing wrong with the commandments.

The "bad" part is that many of us forget that to love our God, we must also love ourselves. We are made in his image!

If we don't value who we are, how can we value the One who made us?

Which leads us to the second commandment: "Love your neighbor as yourself." Again it follows: If we don't see ourselves as lovable and valuable, what must we think about our neighbor?

Remember the JOY acronym? (Now it's your turn to say "*Aha!*") Of course, at first glance, it seems entirely appropriate:

Jesus first;
Others second;
Yourself last.

(Now that I think of it, my brother was its biggest proponent during our childhood: It assured him that he would get the largest piece of chocolate cake when I was serving.)

But now, when I consider the natural order of relationships with our God and with others, I wonder if it is more appropriate to first consider our God and who he is, including all those things we discovered about him in chapter two. Second, we consider who we are as made by a perfect God who does all things well. And third, in celebration of who we are—filled with intrinsic God-given worth—we look at our neighbors and celebrate their value as well.

I haven't come up with an acronym to replace JOY. Instead, I picture a triangle with "Jesus" at the upper angle; "Others" at the left; and "Yourself" at the right angle. I believe it symbolizes a healthier way to consider who we are in relation to God and to others.

It's also interesting to consider that the Greek word for *love* in Matthew 22 ("Love the Lord your God with all your heart and with all your soul and with all your mind") is not *phileo*, which expresses friendly affection, but *agapao*, the commitment of devotion that is directed by the will and can be commanded as a duty.

It follows, then, that loving your neighbor as yourself is a commitment of devotion, a duty.

And to love yourself—so that you can love your neighbor equally—is also a commitment of devotion, a duty, a command!

This is not a comfortable thought.

Somehow, it seems . . . selfish? Potentially self-serving? Self-centered? Heretical?

I've got good news: This love, *agapao*, isn't. (And we'll discuss narcissism in the following section.)

We are not talking about a warm, fuzzy love that is based on emotion. This love elicits a commitment to value the intrinsic worth of our God, ourselves, and others.

It's not a whim to be taken lightly (as *phileo*, or friendly affection, can be). Rather, we are called to commit ourselves to the duty of valuing with every part of our being—*heart, soul, mind* (the Hebrew of Deuteronomy 6:5 adds "*strength*")—our God, others, ourselves.

*Ourselves?*

Does this mean we have God's permission to love/value/be-devoted-to/celebrate-the-worth-of . . . *us?*

No. We don't have his permission.

We have his commandment to do so.

### *The Ugly: Counterfeit Self-Love (Narcissism)*

There is a big difference between valuing ourselves as God's creation and loving ourselves in a "boastful, proud, abusive" manner (2 Tim. 3:2). This is counterfeit self-value and based in self, not God. It is characterized by self-centeredness, self-importance, arrogance, and vainglory. In its extreme, it is known as narcissism.

Narcissism is a personality disorder characterized by extreme self-centeredness and self-absorption with fantasies involving unrealistic goals and excessive need for attention and admiration. The narcissistic personality has difficulty with interpersonal relationships because of a lack of empathy and hypersensitivity to the evaluation of others.[2] The narcissistic personality is characterized by at least five of the following:

- Reacts to criticism with feelings of rage, shame, or humiliation (even if not expressed)
- Interpersonally exploitive: takes advantage of others to achieve her ends
- Has a grandiose sense of self-importance; e.g., exaggerates achievements and talents, expects to be noticed as "special" without appropriate achievement
- Believes that her problems are unique and can only be understood by other "special" people
- Is preoccupied with fantasies of unlimited success, power, brilliance, beauty, or ideal love
- Has a sense of entitlement: unreasonable expectation of especially favorable treatment
- Requires constant attention and admiration; e.g., "fishes" for compliments
- Lack of empathy: inability to recognize how others feel
- Is preoccupied with feelings of envy

Stephen Johnson describes narcissistic people as "too busy proving their worth or, more properly, disproving their worthlessness—to feel the love, appreciation and joy of human relationships."[3]

Even the apostle Paul in writing to young Timothy about "the last days" describes the narcissistic personality:

> People will be lovers of themselves, lovers of money, boastful, proud, abusive, disobedient to their parents, ungrateful, unholy, without love, unforgiving, slanderous, without self-control, brutal, not lovers of the good, treacherous, rash, conceited, lovers of pleasure rather than lovers of God—having a form of godliness but denying its power.
>
> 2 Timothy 3:2–5

While it is true that we are "wonderfully and fearfully made," it is our Creator who deserves the praise, honor, and glory for us, his creation. And we, in humbleness of heart, acknowledge that everything we are, everything we hope to become depends on him, is sustained by him.

So as we prepare to dream, let's make it our earnest prayer that our lives, our dreams, will bring him, not ourselves, glory.

## Soul Famine

Not long ago Dana, a dear and longtime friend, and I got together for a visit. For a special treat, we decided to go to high tea at a beautiful old Pasadena hotel. We settled into some comfy chairs with Earl Grey in our cups and salmon pate and scones on our plates and caught up on the latest news of family and friends.

Then, Dana, knowing I was working on the manuscript for this book, asked how it was going.

"I'm working on a section called 'Soul Famine,'" I said.

She took a deep breath. "Oh, boy. You don't have to explain what that means. I know firsthand."

And she began to tell me about her years in a barren, famine-filled land—not in the middle of the Mojave Desert—but in a frightening place inside herself, a place that had been totally hidden from even her closest friends, a place from which she almost didn't return.

I settled into my chair and listened to her story.

"I married young. I hadn't known Jake long, but from the beginning I was in awe of his tall, dark good looks. He was the silent type. I thought I could draw him out. I had no doubt that our communication would improve once we were married.

"But that was the biggest error I could have made. Because we didn't communicate openly, I *assumed* he wanted all the same things I did—children, a home, pursuit of the educational, cultural, fun things that couples and families do.

"We got married. It didn't take long for me to realize my mistake. His possessiveness began right away. He wanted me to give up my job so that I could be home with him. (He worked afternoons.) When I got pregnant he wanted me to have an abortion. He didn't speak to me for weeks when I refused.

"I wanted to return to school to complete my degree. I had always dreamed of teaching high school art. I had maybe a year to go to get my credential. But it was out of the question. Especially after the kids were born—'after all,' he would tell me, 'you're the one who wanted kids.'

"For a while I found solace in a wonderful, intensive Bible study, one morning a week, he begrudgingly allowed me to attend. But when I was asked to lead a group on an additional morning, he was angry that I would even consider it. I gave it up, feeling that peace in our relationship was more important than doing something that made me happy."

Dana had tears in her eyes as she spoke. I touched her hand. "You don't need to go into all this—" I said.

"No. It's all right. I want to tell my story. Others need to know. Women in our generation were taught to honor and obey—no matter what the cost. Even at church. No one ever said, 'What if that husband is emotionally unhealthy?' Or, 'What if that husband is abusive?'"

I watched Dana as she spoke and thought about all the years I had known her. No one—not even those close to her—would have guessed the pain she had experienced. Dana is a pretty woman, always beautifully dressed with a ready smile. She and her husband seemed to have everything—a lovely home, two fresh-faced kids, a couple of cars, even a private plane for zipping here and there. No one guessed that it was not the perfect life.

Dana went on. "During our first year of marriage, I remember crying myself to sleep at night, thinking, 'I'm going to forget who I really am.' Then the years passed, and I didn't think about it anymore. I just buried myself in the lives of my children and husband. Sure enough, my prophecy was fulfilled. I couldn't remember who I was as an individual.

"Then one summer after we had been married fourteen years, things began unraveling."

She looked pale as the memory came into focus.

"What happened?" I asked. I remembered that a few years earlier Dana had spent several months in and out of hospitals.

"I began experiencing severe chest pains. I thought I was having a heart attack. Then I couldn't breathe. Each attack lasted several minutes. The first few times Jake took me to the emergency room, they ran EKGs, blood tests, the works, but couldn't find anything wrong."

"That must have been frightening."

"It was," she said softly. "I was scared to death. It never occurred to me that it could be emotional; I just felt that the doctors couldn't pinpoint the physical cause. I was sure that with each new attack I was about to die."

I looked at Dana gently. "Did anyone mention that you might be having anxiety attacks?"

"My doctor said I wasn't the type—I was obviously in control of my emotions. I didn't fit the stereotypical pattern of women who were victims of anxiety attacks, or panic attacks."

"How did you feel as the weeks and months wore on?"

She looked almost embarrassed. "It got so bad that I thought I was going crazy. I remember one night in particular. I was lying next to Jake when an attack began. I felt so alone, alienated from God, from everyone—even from myself—whoever that person was."

Dana's eyes were bright with tears again as she continued, and her voice almost a whisper. "I remember feeling that I was in a dark place within my soul. I saw myself as this small being cowering in a corner, covering my head and wishing I were dead."

I took a deep breath, feeling some of Dana's pain as she spoke.

She looked up, her clear gray eyes meeting mine, and smiled. "It was in that desert place that I heard God speak through words of a long-forgotten Bible verse: 'I have not given you the spirit of fear, but of power and love and a sound mind' [see 2 Tim. 1:7 KJV]. I clung to those words as if they had been audibly spoken by God. I no longer felt alone, and I felt a new strength begin to fill me. At that point, I decided to take control. I knew I had a long way to go. But I was determined to find my way out of that empty, dark place."

Our server poured more Earl Grey into our cups, and for a moment neither Dana nor I spoke. Then, as Dana stirred a sugar cube into her tea, I said, "I'm sorry. I had no idea."

She smiled again, this time patting my hand. "Don't apologize. Those events happened more than six years ago. A lot has happened since then."

"Tell me about it." I could tell by the light in her eyes that this would be the happier part of her story.

"I got into counseling. It was a long and complicated process to untie all the emotional knots. But one thing stood out: Through the years I had given up the essence of who I was to take care of the other people in my life.

"I gave and gave and gave, until there was nothing left of myself." She paused. "Talk about—"

"Soul famine," I finished. And Dana nodded.

Dana's story is perhaps extreme, but it still holds elements of a truth that many of us can relate to:

*Number one:* We run the risk of hungering to the point of famine if we're not careful to nurture this being God has commanded us to love—this being that makes up the core of us, body, soul, mind, and spirit.

*Number two:* As a wise woman once told me, if we don't take care of ourselves, who will?

*Number three:* The care and feeding of a hungry soul begins with the simplest common denominator and multiplies from there.

In the following chapter we will examine the care and feeding of those things that make up the core of us—body (the physical), mind (the intellectual), spirit (the emotional), and soul (the spiritual).

~~~

## Reflections

So God created man in his own image,
in the image of God he created him;
male and female he created them.

God saw all that he had made, and it was very good.

GENESIS 1:27, 31

This week, consider with awe the intricacies of your design—physically, intellectually, emotionally, and spiritually. Consider, too, that God created woman as a completion, not as an afterthought, of his fullest self-revelation. Celebrate who you are: woman and child of God, unique and valued. Praise God for who you are in him!

*Dear Lord, may our image of ourselves be that of yours reflected in us. May our self-esteem be based on your value-system, instead of our own. Help us discover—and rejoice in—those things that make us unique.*

# 4

# It's Time to Nurture Ourselves

BREAKFAST:
  ½ grapefruit
  1 piece whole wheat toast
  8 oz. skim milk

LUNCH:
  4 oz. lean breast of chicken
  1 cup steamed zucchini
  1 Oreo cookie
  1 cup herb tea

MIDAFTERNOON
SNACK:
  Rest of package of Oreo
    cookies
  1 quart Rocky Road ice
    cream
  1 jar hot fudge

*DINNER:*
*2 loaves banana bread*
*1 large pepperoni pizza*
*5 Milky Way bars*
*1 entire frozen cheesecake—*
    *eaten directly from the freezer.*

JOEL WELDON

Twenty-some years ago when I was pregnant with my firstborn daughter, I wanted to have the healthiest infant ever born. Adele Davis, a health and nutrition expert, recommended a menu that included a morning "blender" shake made of raw milk, powdered milk, raw eggs (with shells), wheat germ, bananas, lecithin, yeast, and heaven knows what else. Every morning I held my nose and gulped down this terrible-tasting liquid, hoping and praying that this child I carried would benefit from my efforts.

After Melinda was born, I continued with my nutritional mind-set, first breast-feeding, then when the appropriate time came, making all her baby food. Only those foods highest in vitamins and minerals, lowest in fat, and of course no preservatives, slid down my little girl's esophagus.

Then came Amy who spit out anything healthy that touched her tongue. She was one of those children who went straight from breast-feeding to asking for McDonald's fries.

Alas, it seemed we spiraled downward from there. As the family grew and time to cook shrank (you remember, those years of carpooling, ballet lessons, swimming lessons, football games, homework, PTA, and a thousand other things), fast food, high-in-fat, low-in-nutrition, or meals that could be nuked in three minutes became the norm. (I did try to instill within my daughters a love for raw carrots, hoping some vitamins might reach the right places in their little bodies and hoping to alleviate some of my guilt.)

But now, there's no excuse. It's time to think about our own nutritional needs. Especially now. We're entering a time of life that can be enriched immensely through caring for our bodies, especially through proper nutrition and moderate exercise.

## Good Health Equals Good Nutrition

If you are reading this book because you have children of nest-bailing age, you are probably nearing midlife. This means that your nutritional needs are different—perhaps even more important now than ever before. For instance, your calcium needs are climbing to what they were during pregnancy (1,000 to 1,500 milligrams per day).

As we age, it is important to do everything we can to maintain our good health and energy levels. How we feel physically will make a difference in how we feel about dreaming dreams and pursuing our dreams.

Let's take a look at those nutrients that provide the essence of our body's good health: carbohydrates, fats, proteins, vitamins, water, and minerals. All of these work together to provide heat and energy, regulate bodily processes, and provide material for repair and growth. Each nutrient has its own functions, so the food we eat must contain all the nutrients for our bodies to function correctly.

To get a good start on a nutrition plan that will leave you feeling fresh and exhilarated, bear in mind these basic rules established by doctors and nutritionists. (The following suggestions are taken from the goals set by the Senate Committee and from the *Dietary Guidelines for Americans* published jointly by the U.S. Department of Agriculture and the U.S. Department of Health and Human Services.)

- *Increase consumption of complex carbohydrates.* This category includes fruits and vegetables; nuts; legumes such as split peas, lentils, chickpeas, and beans; whole grains such as brown rice, bulgar, and buckwheat; and whole-grain products such as whole-wheat bread, whole-grain crackers, bran cereals, non-instant oatmeal, and oat bran.

- *Reduce consumption of refined sugars.* This category includes processed foods that list sugars as first, second, or third ingredients. "Natural" sugars such as honey, barley malt, maple syrup, apple concentrate, and molasses are only slightly better for you and should be eaten only in small quantities.
- *Reduce overall fat consumption.* Foods to cut down on include fatty cuts of meat, processed meats (cold cuts, sausages), deep-fried foods, butter, margarine, mayonnaise, high-fat cheeses, pastries, chips, and other snack foods. Good substitutes include fish, poultry without the skin, low-fat dairy products, and vegetable proteins such as grains and beans.
- *Change the ratio of saturated to unsaturated fats, reducing the use of saturated fats.* Saturated fats are generally solid at room temperature and include animal fats, hydrogenated (hardened) vegetable fats, and coconut and palm oils. Unsaturated fats are liquid at room temperature and include vegetable or nut oils. Saturated fats raise cholesterol levels while unsaturated fats lower them. Monounsaturated fats, such as peanut or olive oil, are liquid at room temperature but solidify easily with refrigeration. Monounsaturates have no effect on (or may even lower) cholesterol levels and can be used in cooking because they remain stable at high temperatures. The fats in fish contain omega-3 fatty acids, which actually lower cholesterol and triglyceride levels in the blood.
- *Reduce sodium consumption.* Eat only small quantities of salt-cured foods, most condiments, salty snack foods, soy sauce, foods containing monosodium glutamate (MSG), most canned vegetables and soups, and any processed food in which salt or sodium is high on the

list of ingredients. Watch your use of salt in cooking and at the table. Keep in mind, though, that some sodium is essential for our body's well-being.

## A Word about Carbohydrates

Carbohydrates should provide 50 percent or more of our energy needs and supply the glucose necessary for brain function. Adequate carbohydrate intake keeps the body from using protein as an energy source so that protein can be conserved for body-building functions.

Carbohydrates are usually divided into two categories: simple and complex. Simple carbohydrates are sugars such as table sugar, honey, and the sugar in fruits (glucose and fructose). Complex carbohydrates are starches such as grains, starchy vegetables, fruits, and beans. All sugars and starches are converted by digestion into a simple sugar called glucose, which is released into the bloodstream. However, the glucose from starches is digested and absorbed more slowly than that from sugar, avoiding the rapid rise and fall of blood sugar that can come from eating too many simple sugars at one time.

Whole foods with complex carbohydrates such as grains also furnish essential nutrients and fiber, while simple carbohydrates such as sugar and refined flour tend to be empty calorie foods—they supply too many calories for the nutrients they provide. White flour loses twenty-three vitamins and minerals in the refining process and is then labeled "enriched" with only four replaced.

### Choosing Our Foods

Nutritionists traditionally divide foods into four groups: (1) fruits and vegetables; (2) dairy products; (3) breads and cereals; and (4) meats and other protein foods. The following serving suggestions provide a flexible and healthy menu for meeting our nutritional needs:

- *Vegetables:* 2 to 5 servings (one serving equals ½ cup). Includes all fresh, frozen, or canned vegetables. Remember, the deeper the color of the vegetable, the higher the vitamin A content, so tip the balance in favor of dark green leafy and yellow/orange vegetables.

- *Fruit:* 1 to 4 servings (one serving equals one average-size fruit, or ½ cup). Includes all unsweetened fruit: fresh, frozen, canned, dried, or juiced. Whole, raw fruit is generally the most nutritious. Include a vitamin C fruit or vegetable source daily.

- *Dairy products:* 1 to 3 servings (one serving equals one cup of liquid such as milk or yogurt, or 1 to 1½ ounces of cheese). Includes milk, yogurt, all cheeses, ice milk, or ice cream—though substituting low-fat dairy products is probably more beneficial.

- *Whole grains, including bread and cereal:* 3 to 6 servings (one serving equals ½ cup of grain or cereal, or one slice of bread). Includes all whole grains—rice, barley, millet, cracked wheat, corn; whole-grain breads and cereals—oatmeal, bran, shredded wheat; whole-grain crackers, pasta, and tortillas. If you are not used to whole grains, start gradually to substitute them for white-flour products and eat only as much as your digestive system can comfortably handle.

- *Protein:* 2 to 3 servings (one serving equals approximately 3 ounces of cooked lean meat, chicken, or fish, 5 ounces of tofu, 2 large eggs, or 1 cup cooked beans). Protein is the second most plentiful substance in our bodies. It is important for the growth, development, and repair of all body tissues. Animal proteins from foods such as meats, poultry, fish, dairy products, and eggs contain all the amino acids in adequate amounts and are therefore "complete proteins." Many vegetables, grains, beans, nuts, seeds, and other complex carbohydrates contain proteins but are "incomplete" by themselves and have to be combined to have sufficient amounts of all the amino acids. Combined vegetable proteins have the advantages of being lower in fat, high in fiber and minerals, and generally lower in cost than complete proteins.

- *Essential fatty acids:* 1 to 2 tablespoons per day in salad dressing or cooking. This is not really a food group, but because fats are part of the basic structure of every cell, we do need small amounts of oil and fat in our diet for good health.

- *Water,* although not a nutrient, is the most important element for life and is frequently overlooked. Our bodies are made mostly of water, which is vital to maintain life and health. Water is essential for proper functioning of the kidneys and bowels and is an important vehicle for disposing of poisonous substances. It is the basic transport system of the body, moving all nutrients, hormones, blood cells, waste products, and oxygen through the body. As we age, our body's ability to control fluid balance becomes less efficient. Most of us need six to eight cups of water daily, and more in some circumstances. Coffee and other caffeinated beverages actually push fluids and minerals out of our systems and should be avoided.

- *Fiber,* also not a nutrient, is nonetheless a necessary component of a well-balanced diet. Fiber serves primarily as a vehicle for holding water, binding both toxic and essential nutrients, and providing the soft bulk that absorbs body waste. Because of these properties, fiber helps our intestines work more smoothly.

### Our Special Need for Calcium

Adequate daily calcium intake is vital throughout our life span. The USRDA remains at 800 milligrams per day, but surveys show that most women consume barely half that amount. The following chart lists current recommendations:

| Age | Milligrams per Day |
| --- | --- |
| 9 to 19 | 1200 |
| If pregnant | 1500–2000 |
| If breast-feeding | 2200 |
| 20 to 50 (premenopausal) | 1000 |
| Postmenopausal or for early natural or surgical menopause | 1500 |

A thousand milligrams of calcium can be obtained in one day by eating all of the following:

- 2 half-cup servings of cooked green vegetables
- 1 ounce of cheese
- 2 cups of skim milk

Adding a corn muffin, a serving of sardines or yogurt, and increasing the two green vegetables to one-cup servings will increase the calcium to 1500 mg. for the day.[1]

Other food sources of calcium include:

| Food | Portion | Calcium (Approx. mg.) |
| --- | --- | --- |
| **Dairy** | | |
| American cheese | 2 oz. | 348 |
| Cheddar cheese | 2 oz. | 408 |
| Cottage cheese, 2% fat | 1 cup | 160 |
| Mozzarella cheese | 2 oz. | 320 |
| Ricotta cheese, part skim | ½ cup | 337 |
| Milk, low fat | 1 cup | 310 |
| Yogurt | 8 oz. | 415 |
| **Non-Dairy** | | |
| *Nuts and Beans:* | | |
| Almonds, chopped | ⅓ cup | 100 |
| Chickpeas, dried | ¼ cup | 75 |

*Fish:*

| | | |
|---|---|---|
| Salmon, sockeye-drained | | |
| solids | 3 oz. | 275 |
| Sardines, Atlantic-drained | | |
| solids | 3 oz. | 371 |

*Vegetables:*

| | | |
|---|---|---|
| Broccoli, fresh cooked | 1 cup | 250 |
| Collard greens, fresh | | |
| cooked | 1 cup | 178 |
| Kale, fresh cooked | 1 cup | 210 |

*Grain Sweeteners:*

| | | |
|---|---|---|
| Blackstrap molasses | 1 tbls. | 140 |

These foods are good sources of calcium, but many other foods can contribute to your overall calcium intake. It pays to be a label reader: nutrition information on food labels should list the calcium content.

### A Word about Crash Dieting

If you are tempted to seek that inner-svelte self that perhaps existed twenty-five years ago (or never stepped out from beneath its padding), think twice about fad or crash dieting. Consider the consequences.

Because they offer so little in balanced nutrition, crash diets can seriously weaken your muscles. Even after a short time, muscle tissue can no longer efficiently process calcium, according to studies done at the University of Toronto. If you attempt this kind of diet, your body will not be able to function properly. It will slow down (simulating starvation) to conserve energy.

Women shouldn't eat fewer than 1,200 calories a day. According to diet and nutrition experts at Stanford University, you can't get all the nutrients you need if you eat less than that. Diets in the 800-calorie range may pose a particular health threat, which can result in a breakdown in heart muscle.

If your health is at risk due to being overweight, seek assistance from a medical doctor, and stay away from fad dieting.

## Good Health Equals Exercise

I've good news and bad news about our need for exercise. First the good news: *Women who are active and who exercise suffer fewer headaches and less chronic back pain, stiffness, painful joints, irregularity, and insomnia.* They report renewed energy and enjoyment of life. Inactivity causes depression, poor circulation, weak muscles, stiff joints, shortness of breath, loss of bone mass, and fatigue.

Fatigue is directly related to lack of oxygen. If your body isn't exercised regularly, it probably doesn't use oxygen very efficiently. Your muscles need oxygen or they don't work as long or as hard as they should. The result of all this inactivity: When you need muscle power, you don't get it, and you tire quickly.

Remember, it will be hard to get started doing anything—let alone pursuing dreams—if you're tired all the time.

Now the bad news: *Exercise is boring. Exercise is time consuming. Exercise is just plain ol' not fun.* But the benefits of increased activity far outweigh the negatives. And when it comes right down to it, patterns adopted today will affect the strength and agility of our bodies tomorrow and in the years to come. Regardless of what our exercise patterns have been in the past, it's not too late to change. Health experts tell us that it takes sixty to ninety days of repeated activity for newly adopted patterns to become habits. So, think of the consequences . . . and the benefits. The time to begin is now.

Believe me, you will be glad you did!

Consider taking just fifteen to twenty minutes a day to devote yourself to new energy and greater vitality through a consistent and increasingly vigorous regimen of stretching and strengthening your limbs, correcting your posture, and conditioning your cardiovascular system.

### Something Good to Consider about Who We Are

Many women—even godly women who understand that they were created by a perfect God—hate their bodies. We may avoid looking at ourselves in the mirror or doing anything physical, especially if it's in front of other people. Unfortunately, that kind of thinking makes us even more inactive.

A Christian therapist who conducts therapy groups for overweight women recently reported that once her clients begin to exercise, attitudes change and self-esteem soars. As the women see their strength and endurance building, it forces them to focus on something other than how their bodies look. They begin to celebrate the beautiful function and movement of their bodies, something of God's creation, their own creation, that they had never before considered.

The therapist's experience corresponds with research that has found that exercise is an antidote to depression and can even raise the mood of nondepressed people. One of the most interesting findings of the latest research is that it's the act of exercising, not fitness, that creates the mood-raising benefits.

A study done at the Institute for Aerobics Research in Dallas, Texas, reported a similar finding related to longevity. The study revealed that even a slight increase in exercise, a half-hour brisk walk every day, can significantly reduce our risk of dying from heart disease, cancer, and other killer diseases.

### Points to Ponder Before We Begin

#### Have Fun!

Yeah, right. (I can hear the groans now.)

But hold on for just a moment before skipping to the next section. Exercise *can* be fun—and rewarding, as we've just seen. So if running hurts your knees and a stationary bike makes your eyes glaze over with boredom, let's consider other options.

How about line dancing? Many communities offer adult education dancing classes, including the latest dance crazes. Or you might want to invest in a video tape and try dancing in the privacy of your own home, especially if you decide to try bellydancing the way a friend of mine did recently.

You might want to play tennis, though make sure your partner is no more adept than you are at the sport. Otherwise, you'll spend more time chasing the ball than hitting it.

Or how about biking? Or rollerblading? (Not something I would try, but I have a friend who rollerblades with her grandchildren.)

Actually, my favorite exercise is a brisk walk. I live in a mountainous area so the constant pull on my muscles as I walk up and down the inclines is invigorating. There are more benefits to walking than just physical, and we'll talk more about those later.

My second favorite is riding my stationary bike *with* my Discman headphones securely in place. With CDs spinning, I can laugh with Garrison Keillor as he tells of the folks in his hometown or I sweat with Zubin Mehta as he leads the L.A. Philharmonic during the Three Tenors concert at Dodger Stadium. Books on tape can also add a wonderful dimension to an otherwise boring-beyond-belief activity.

No matter which exercise you choose, always warm up with five minutes of stretching, slow-walking, or any activity that gently accelerates heart rate, breathing, and circulation.

It's important that you don't set yourself up for failure by setting unrealistic goals. If you begin an overly ambitious exercise plan, it may last a couple of weeks, then you'll drop it. (I know because I've done it.) Rather, do something moderate, something that will easily fit into your schedule. Most studies that examine the physical and psychological health benefits of exercise have found that a little goes a long way. Take a look at what you can do and what you can sustain.

### Celebrate!

As you exercise, celebrate the function and movement, the growing strength and flexibility of the wonderful body that God created—just for you. Keep in mind that this is a time of life to experiment, to try new and enjoyable activities, just for you.

## Nurturing the Intellectual Us

When I mentioned intellectual nurturing to Dr. Dennis Hill, a prominent neurologist from North Carolina, Dr. Hill (who is also my brother) had this to say: "Until recently it was thought that the human brain had reached its ultimate capacity by a person's late teens. But now studies have proven that the brain can continue expanding, growing, increasing in capacity with 'exercise'—just like any other muscle in the body."

"You mean a person can get smarter as they get older? *A lot* older? As in *middle age?*" I asked incredulously.

"Yes," he said. "But it depends on how the person 'exercises' his or her brain."

(I was a little uncomfortable discussing a person's mental capacity with my brother, the *neurologist,* but I forged ahead.) "So if a person does crossword puzzles, plays chess, or reads, instead of watching soaps, the brain will actually grow?"

"That's right," he said. "Over time the intellect actually expands to meet the challenge."

"Wow." That from me. (Notice the vocabulary. That's why *he's* the doctor.)

*Brain exercise!*

Who would have thought?

When we look in the mirror we may see sagging muscles in every other part of our anatomy, but behind those beautiful, bright eyes staring back at us rests a muscle that will never grow flabby, unless we allow it.

Samuel Johnson, a wise man who lived in the eighteenth century, said, "A generous and elevated mind is distinguished by nothing more certainly than an eminent degree of curiosity."

*Curiosity?*

Isn't that the trait of kittens and little children? Yes. But it's also that precious and rare quality that can create in us "a generous and elevated mind."

Let's take a look at those things that might pique our curiosity. Open your journal and think about the subjects and people that have interested you. These may be curiosities you've had for years but have just never taken the time to pursue. Or they may be completely new thoughts. Take your time and consider the wealth of offerings. Then . . .

1. *Select a subject:* What are you interested in? Your list may be drawn from broad areas such as music, art, history, philosophy, politics; or it may include specific interests such as birds, ballet, the stock market, or meteorology.

Whatever subject you choose, delve into it with gusto. Dig deep, far beneath the surface. Have fun with your discoveries. Are you interested in birds? Go beyond the creation of a bird sanctuary (with bird feeders, bird baths, or bird houses) in your yard. Buy books on bird identification. Take an ornithology class. Join a bird watching group. Volunteer to help them do their annual count of a given species in your hometown.

Let your curiosity expand other areas of your life. Don't just admire a tree, find out what kind it is. Notice the shape of its leaves and their color. Why do they contain the colors they do? Is this kind of tree native to the area? If not, who introduced it? Pioneers? Which century? From what continent?

When I compiled my list of curiosities a few years ago, word studies landed at the top. Since then, I have been delighted to make the pursuit of odd and curious dictionaries a kind of hobby. So whatever your interest is, be it mainstream or off the beaten track, go for it!

2. *Select a person:* Who would you like to get acquainted with? He or she may be a historical figure (Winston Churchill, Abraham Lincoln, Eleanor Roosevelt, Albert Schweitzer, Marian Anderson, or Robert Frost) or someone contemporary whom you admire (Edith Schaeffer, Margaret Thatcher, Mother Teresa).

Not long ago, after hearing an intriguing piece of music from the Middle Ages, I became interested in the life of a rather obscure historical figure, Hildegard of Bingen, a twelfth-century abbess. Curious, I purchased the CD "A Feather on the Breath of God," featuring sequences and hymns written and composed by the abbess.

I was fascinated to find that Hildegard, born in 1098, became one of the most celebrated women of her age as a visionary, naturalist, playwright, poetess, and composer. In 1141, having become an abbess, she saw tongues of flame descend from the heavens and settle upon her. Afterward she devoted herself to a life of intense and passionate creativity. She produced two books on natural history and medicine and a morality play, which predates all other works in that genre by some one hundred years.

Throughout her lifetime, Hildegard was involved in politics and diplomacy; her friendship and advice were sought by popes, emperors, kings, archbishops, abbots, and abbesses with whom she corresponded.

Even today—nearly a thousand years later—Hildegard's love for God shines through her writings. As an example, these words from *O ignis spiritus:*

> O fire of the comforting Spirit,
> life of the life of all Creation,
> you are holy in quickening all Kind.
> You are holy in anointing the dangerously stricken;
> you are holy in wiping
> the reeking wound.

O breath of holiness
O fire of love
O sweet draught in the breast
and flooding of the heart
in the good aroma of virtues. . . .
Whence praise be to you
who are the sound of praise
and bliss of life,
hope and richest gift
giving the rewards of light.

How I rejoice in the riches that are mine for having become acquainted with such a woman of God!

Last, there is no greater mental exercise than reading. Yet, as with so many exercise programs, we can place it last after the other things that crowd into our days.

Beginning now, make reading a priority. Let your curiosity be your guide to opening worlds of wonder and delight. Even if you read only twenty minutes when you go to bed at night—*just do it!* (Then fall asleep picturing those little brain cells jumping up and down, lifting barbells, and moving to step aerobics.)

## Nurturing the Emotional Us

My friend Rachel, mother of three nest-escapees (one married, two others away at college), recently told me about a trip she took, alone. (Her first *completely* alone—no kids, husband, pets.) She flew from Southern California, where she lives with her husband, to Massachusetts. Having just begun working as a professional photographer, she was on her first photo shoot.

Rachel finished the job in fewer days than she had expected, so she decided to drive along the coast, spend time at a couple of bed-and-breakfasts, and immerse herself in the beautiful eastern land- and seascapes.

"I couldn't believe the joy I felt," Rachel said. "Of course, at first I was nervous. I hadn't even rented a car alone before. But after some friends recommended the B & Bs, and I got on the road, a real peace settled in. Even God's presence seemed more tangible than I had ever experienced.

"For a few days I wandered up the coast, stopped to shoot some pictures and to simply drink in God's beauty. I was no one's mother or wife. I felt anonymous, but not in a negative sense. It was tremendously positive."

I wanted to hear more about this. "Anonymous?" I prodded.

She nodded. "Maybe it was because the place was unfamiliar to me; everything I experienced was out of the context of family, friends, or other responsibilities. I had nothing around me that 'told' who I was, even to me."

Her eyes softened. "I discovered a place inside that I had forgotten existed. I'm sure God knew it was there, but during those few days, I was able to find it."

"What place was that?"

"That place where I am separate from everyone else." She looked at me solemnly. "I'd been connected to my husband and kids for so long, I'd almost forgotten what it's like to be alone. And who I am when I am by myself."

"How about the guilt you felt?"

Rachel looked at me, surprised, for just a moment. Then she laughed. "How did you know?"

"Because we moms have a knack for putting family ahead of ourselves. Sometimes it begins before motherhood. It's only natural that we're hit by a ton of guilt when we step out of that role."

Rachel agreed. "I know what you mean. I remember when Keith and I announced our engagement, twenty-seven years ago. I'll never forget my mother's words. She said, 'All you're thinking about is your own happiness. You don't care about anyone else.' The funny thing is, when she said it, her words made sense. All of my life, I had been taught to put others' happiness first."

She went on to tell how much her mother loves Keith. She also said that she now understands that her mother was projecting her own frustrations of giving up her happiness for others. Her daughter should be required to do no less.

"That's why guilt raises its ugly head when you do something that makes you—*just you*—happy."

Rachel grinned. "Yeah. Big time."

We may feel undeserving of pursuits we see as "self-indulgent." These activities may be as extensive as a short trip alone (such as my friend Rachel's) or as simple as a long soak in a bubble bath. We aren't used to doing things entirely for ourselves, for the benefit of no earthly being other than us.

The thought of "such selfishness" can be uncomfortable. When confronted with the option of doing for ourselves or doing for others, an internal voice clears its throat and whispers, *Isn't that a little selfish of you, dear?*

We have seen the benefits of caring for ourselves physically. An important part of that care includes taking time out to renew our energies for the journey ahead, especially as we look forward to preparing to dream. This is no more selfish or self-indulgent than plugging in a laptop computer for battery recharging.

Immerse yourself in art or music; take a "music bath," as Oliver Wendell Holmes counseled: "Take a music bath once or twice a week for a few seasons, and you will find that it is to the soul what a water-bath is to the body." Or walk slowly through God's creation in an arboretum or other public gardens, taking time to drink in the creamy pastels of a newborn rose or to observe the turning of an ivy leaf in the breeze. Drive to the beach if you live near a body of water, and simply sit and watch the waves, the gulls, and sandpipers. Breathe deeply and let your senses take in the feel of the breeze on your face, the touch of sun on your shoulders, and the sand between your toes. Clear your mind of everything except those things you feel and see.

In this age of power-showers, we tend to forget the therapeutic effects of bathing. And I don't mean just a tub full of water. I mean a Real Bath: scented water, bubbles, soft music, candlelight. The Real Bath lasts an hour or more. Take the telephone off the hook and hang a Do Not Disturb sign on the bathroom door. Then lie back and clear your mind of all else but the feel of the water, the scent of the bubbles, and the sounds of a Beethoven sonata in your candlelit sanctuary. Talk about the pause that refreshes! This, in my opinion, is head and shoulders above all the rest. (So to speak.) How better to bring peace to our spirits and rest to our bodies. We can agree with Proverbs 14:30: "A heart at peace gives life to the body."

Don't forget the benefits of laughter. In Proverbs 17:22 we read, "A cheerful heart is good medicine, but a crushed spirit dries up the bones," and in Proverbs 15:15, "The cheerful heart has a continual feast." Norman Cousins, one-time editor of the prestigious *Saturday Review*, discovered the therapeutic benefits of laughter after he was given little hope for a cure from a painful inflammatory disease of his spine and joints. He found that ten minutes of belly laughter gave him two hours of pain-free sleep. He programmed laughter into his life, and his condition began to improve.

Cousins shared his experiment with health-care facilities that dealt with patients experiencing severe pain. The results were so impressive that dozens of similar programs were set up across the country. In quoting the Russian novelist Dostoyevsky, Cousins once said,

> If you wish to glimpse inside a human soul and get to know a man, don't bother analyzing his ways of being silent, of talking, of weeping, or seeing how much he is moved by noble ideas; you'll get better results if you just watch him laugh. If he laughs well, he's a good man. . . . All I claim to know, is that laughter is the most reliable gauge of human nature.[2]

## Nurturing the Spiritual Us

> Not merely an absence of noise,
> Real Silence begins when a reasonable being
> withdraws from the noise
> in order to find peace and
> order in his inner sanctuary.
> The exodus from slavery
> toward the possession of the Kingdom.
>
> PETER MINARD

Consider again Mother Teresa's words: "God speaks in the silence of our hearts." Depending on the intensity of your church involvement, by this time—just considering your hands-on motherhood years—you have spent somewhere between three thousand and five thousand hours in Sunday school and church. We took to heart (and still do) the admonition, "Forsake not the gathering together . . ." and generously gave of our time teaching Sunday school classes and VBS, leading children's choirs, helping with Christmas productions, and counseling at summer church camp. Add to that time at home spent raising families in the fear and admonition of God, and usually there was little spiritual energy left for one-on-one time with our Lord.

Guess what?

It's time to seek him.

Alone.

In the silence of our hearts.

We're on a journey of discovery. But without discovering who we are in Christ, we'll never arrive at our destination. Thomas Merton expresses it this way in *Thoughts in Solitude:*

> We find God in our own being, which is the mirror of God. But how do we find our being?
>
> Actions are the doors and windows of being. Unless we act we have no way of knowing what we are. And the

experience of our existence is impossible without some experience of knowing or some experience of experience.[3]

The time for us to act is now. It's time to draw away, alone, into that quiet place where God can impress on our hearts and minds those secrets he wants us to learn—about himself, about us in him. Thomas Merton goes on to say:

> He waits to communicate Himself to me in a way that I can never express to others or even think about coherently to myself. *I must desire it in silence. It is for this that I must leave all things.*[4] (emphasis mine)

Church retreats are wonderful: There are couples' retreats, adult Sunday school class retreats, church board retreats, ladies' retreats, all spiritually uplifting ways to meet Christ away from familiar surroundings.

But hardly places of solitude. Hardly places where one can be alone with God for longer than a few hours at a time.

Have you ever considered taking a spiritual retreat alone? *Completely* alone?

This might be a scary thought. But it is only when we are completely alone that we can know God more intimately through prayer and study.

I have found that one of the most fulfilling studies during a spiritual retreat is that of the attributes of God. God himself tells us, "Acquaint now thyself with him, and be at peace; thereby good shall come unto thee" (Job 22:21 KJV), and "Be still, and know that I am God" (Ps. 46:10).

A wonderful resource for that study is *Nave's Topical Bible*. Find the section on God, Jesus, and the Holy Spirit. I promise: You will be blessed as you read! J. I. Packer's book *Knowing God* is another source of delight and inspiration, and its reading will bring a precious awareness of who God is and who we are in him. Companion readings might be *The Attributes of God* by Arthur Pink and *The Knowledge of the Holy* by A. W. Tozer.[5]

Time alone with God is important for your spiritual nurturing. If you have not already discovered the riches of meeting him one-on-one, try it today. Just set aside fifteen minutes. Quiet yourself before him. Clear your mind of all else. Picture Christ waiting for you to join him, just as someone awaits a cherished friend.

You are that friend.

Tell him how glad you are to be with him.

Then be silent. Let only your heart speak in adoring silence. Consider his majesty.

Now let your lips praise him. You might try singing soft words of praise such as in the chorus *I Love You, Lord,* by Laurie Klein.[6]

Think about how God rejoices over you with singing.

Thank him for loving you that much!

Thank him for creating you to be just who you are. Unlike any other of his created beings. You are unique.

Spend a few moments in silent praise for the Creator. For his creation.

Bring your family members before him. One by one, name them. Know that he cares for each one more than you do.

And bring him your concerns. Ask him for guidance—to be with you in any decisions you have to make this day.

Leave your burdens with him. (He's asked you to.)

Ask Jesus to help you this day . . . and the days ahead as you journey down this new path of dream discovery.

Think again about who your God is: almighty, compassionate, merciful, all-knowing, faithful, forgiving, just. Remember: Nothing is too hard for him! He is the friend who remains with you—in you—even as this quiet time comes to a close.

> True silence is the rest of the mind;
> it is to the spirit what sleep is to the body,
> nourishment and refreshment.
>
> WILLIAM PENN

## Reflections

Taste and see that the Lord is good.

PSALM 34:8

This week, examine your fitness for the journey ahead. Consider any changes you should make in your diet or exercise program. Take time to follow the path of an intellectual curiosity. Bathe yourself in music, laughter, and simple joys. Celebrate your relationship with the One who loves you: He is your Nourishment, your Bread of Life, your Living Water. Spend time alone with him each day, and taste of his goodness.

*Dear Jesus, ready us for our journey of dream discovery. Help us see those things in our lives that need to be changed. Toughen us. Deepen us. Open us to your possibilities.*

# 5

# Expanding the Comfort Zone

*In the heating and air conditioning trade, the point on the thermostat in which neither heating nor cooling must operate—around 72 degrees—is called the "comfort zone." It's also known as "the dead zone."*

RUSSELL BISHOP

Many of us find that we have lived within certain parameters, done things a certain way for such a long period of time that discomfort—sometimes extreme discomfort—sets in when we change those parameters. As someone has pointed out, even convicts are uncomfortable when released from prison.

The barriers that can keep us from growing are very real: fear, guilt, unworthiness, discouragement, and procrastination. In the pages that follow, we will look at how each of these affects our choices. We will explore how we can change the way we view these barriers and how we can expand our comfort zones—in spite of them.

## What Exactly Is a "Comfort Zone"?

We have lived four decades (plus or minus a few years) within the parameters of our own thoughts and actions, our own area of personal comfort. Those things we do or thoughts we think have been acted or thought often enough to feel comfortable. Anything new (not previously thought about or acted on often enough to be comfortable) lies outside our comfort zone.

As an example, suppose I were to give you an airline ticket to a Third World country. In fact, you've never traveled internationally before. Yet here you are with your ticket to someplace you've never been. You can't speak the language. You are unfamiliar with the country and know nothing of its culture. You know no one at your destination.

What if I told you that hundreds of malnourished children in this impoverished country would benefit if you would go? And that they are counting on you to help them? How would you feel? Uncomfortable? Overwhelmed?

Close your eyes. Picture yourself on the tarmac, looking up at the cockpit of the plane: You see the pilot staring intently at a map, turning it from side to side, scratching his head. Now how do you feel? Fearful? Unworthy? ("Who am *I* thinking I could help anyway?")

Maybe you've dreamed of being an international photojournalist, and this is your chance of a lifetime. Your story could bring the plight of these children to the attention of the whole world. The resulting global response could drastically change the living conditions within the country.

Adventure, intrigue, life-changing encounters will be yours if you simply board the plane.

But again you hesitate, this time feeling something akin to guilt. Guilt for pursuing a dream that is yours alone after so many years of nurturing the dreams of others. Guilt because you *can't* move past the previously mentioned barriers.

What if I made a slightly different offer to you? You will return to school and complete a degree in journalism. You will train with a world-class photographer. You will complete an internship with an international relief and development organization. You will receive the help of a mentor along the way.

Then I again offer you the airline ticket to the impoverished Third World country, reminding you of the hundreds of children who will be helped if you go.

What will your answer be?

If you are still in the "I can't" category, you may be feeling uncomfortable because of other barriers: low self-worth and discouragement. (As in, "Are you kidding? I couldn't get past getting my degree. I flunked out of college twenty-five years ago!" Or, "Why would a world-class photographer want to work with me? What do I have to offer?" Or, "The way the job market is today, it wouldn't matter if I had three degrees. I wouldn't get hired.")

A word here about the barriers of low self-esteem and discouragement: Henry Ford said, "If you think you can do a thing or think you can't do a thing, you're right." He's correct. If we think we can't do something, we don't spend time thinking about it or acting on it. Therefore, we're right. We can't do it. It's a self-fulfilling prophecy.

Now think about moving past the "I can't" of the comfort zone. Picture yourself photographing a child from our fictitious Third World country, writing about her plight, drawing the attention of donors to help alleviate her hunger and that of hundreds of her neighbors. You've overcome the barriers and moved outside your comfort zone. You are living your dream. And you are finding adventure, excitement, satisfaction, and a world of wonder you never before knew existed.

But back to the nuts and bolts of the comfort zone. Have you ever heard someone say, "I can't do that. It feels uncomfortable"? And have you noticed that "discomfort" (for most people) seems to be more than a reason—it's an accepted fact for not doing something?

The walls that make up our comfort zone are the primary reasons we back away from pursuing our dreams. These barriers include feelings such as fear, guilt, unworthiness, hurt feelings, and anger. When we feel any one of them, or a combination of several, we are uncomfortable. And when we back away from our cherished dreams because of these barriers, another wall, even higher, deeper, and wider, settles in. And that wall is discouragement.

> You have to leave the city of your comfort and go into the wilderness of your intuition. What you'll discover will be wonderful. What you'll discover will be yourself.
>
> ALAN ALDA

Let's take a closer look at those emotions that comprise the walls of the "city" of our comfort zone.

## Fear

> You gain strength, courage, and confidence by every experience in which you really stop to look fear in the face. You are able to say to yourself, "I lived through this horror. I can take the next thing that comes along." You must do the thing you think you cannot do.
>
> ELEANOR ROOSEVELT

Fear is perhaps the most common limiting emotion experienced by humankind. We understand it and have encountered it under many different names: alarm, anxiety, dread, horror, terror, misgiving, trepidation, foreboding, distress, uneasiness, phobia, panic . . . and the list goes on. It can strike us in the mind—then travel quickly to the stomach or the lower abdomen. The pulse quickens. Breathing accelerates. Senses sharpen. We agree with Shakespeare's assessment of fear: "Of all base passions, fear is the most accursed." And he also points out that we are often "distilled almost to jelly with the act of fear." Sophocles said, "To him who is in fear, everything rustles." And Bertrand Russell wrote, "Fear is the main source of superstition, and one of the main sources of cruelty."

Fear is often the emotion we feel in addition to other negative emotions: We are *afraid* to feel guilt. We are *afraid* to feel uncomfortable. We are *afraid* to feel pain. Even when we feel fear, we are *afraid* to feel it! Or, as said by Montaigne in the sixteenth century (and many others since), "The thing I fear most is fear." It's also that feeling producing the emotional climate for anxiety and panic attacks.

Someone has given fear an acronym: False Expectation Appearing Real. Even Aristotle described fear as "pain arising from the anticipation of evil."

And so we back away from the thing we fear, never to discover whether or not our projection was accurate. We may even heave a huge sigh of relief, never realizing that had we taken the courage to journey to our fear's center, we would have found . . . nothing. Nothing but fear itself. Just fear, afraid of itself. Someone has called it one of the greatest (and cruelest) jokes played on humankind.

I've got good news! As with many emotions that we may perceive as harmful, fear can actually work *for* us. We've all heard of stories such as that of the young mother who, in a burst of adrenaline, lifted a three-thousand-pound car to release her child trapped beneath it. Of course the mother acted without an analysis of her fear; she simply reacted to the immediacy of the need. Yet the unplanned channeling of energy was there when she needed it, enabling her to act with superhuman strength.

Circumstances such as this are extreme. But think about the implications: Fear can and does work *for* us. When we are afraid, we receive an extra burst of energy and a sharpening of our senses. Into the blood stream flow adrenaline, glucose, and a host of other energy-producing chemicals. The result? Our bodies become poised and ready to act.

What do we need when we are faced with a new situation, real or imagined? More energy. In a new situation, all our senses need to be fine-tuned, in prime condition to bring to us all the information we need. This is exactly what happens when our bodies kick into a fear mode. Our sharpened senses, sensitivity, and heightened awareness (all begotten of fear) help us process the information more quickly and efficiently.

As we move forward toward living our dreams, we need to rethink our attitudes about fear. Reprogram your thoughts (once you know something is not physically dangerous) and begin to break old habits, using these steps:

1. *Feel* the fear and find it's a phantom.
2. *Do* the thing you fear.
3. *Use* the energy from your fear.
4. *Write* on your heart: "Do not be afraid, for I am with you, I will bless you" (Gen. 26:24).

Take out your journal and write the heading, "I have not given you the spirit of fear, but of power and love and a sound mind" (2 Tim. 1:7 KJV, paraphrased).

Next, write down your fear. (Just pick one for now.) Close your eyes and imagine yourself doing that which you fear.

How do you feel? Record those feelings in the journal.

Take a quick assessment of your physical reaction to your fear. Sometimes even imagining a fearful circumstance can quicken the pulse or cause butterflies in the stomach.

Now, in your mind, turn those reactions into positive energies and continue to do that which you fear.

Next, write in your journal the verse quoted above (Gen. 26:24). Whisper God's words, "Do not be afraid, for I am with you," and understand that they are his words for *you*. He *knows* what you feel, and he is there *with* you in your fear.

Thank him for being with you. Ask him to help you work through your fears. And remember these words of pilot Eddie Rickenbacker: "Courage is doing what you're afraid to do. There can be no courage unless you're scared."

## Guilt

> Guilt is never a rational thing; it distorts all the faculties of the human mind, perverts them, it leaves a man no longer in the free use of his reason, it puts him into confusion.
>
> EDMUND BURKE

Guilt is an emotion; guilt is also a condition. As Christians we often get the emotion mixed up with the condition.

Guilt, the emotion, is self-judgment. Guilt, the condition ("All have sinned and fall short of the glory of God," Rom. 3:23) is God-judgment, for which he has provided atonement through his Son Jesus and from which he lifts us with his arm of grace.

For the purposes of this book, let's take a closer look at guilt, the emotion.

First of all, this guilt stems from the anger we feel toward ourselves when we judge ourselves to have done something "wrong." The problem is, many of us have picked up views through the years that have become habits. B. F. Skinner writes, "Society attacks early, when the individual is helpless." It's possible that we may not be able to remember exactly why something feels "right" or "wrong." Some of us may have suffered childhood trauma that skewed a healthy sense of "right" for us. For instance, we may be filled with guilt feelings telling us that we shouldn't be too successful. "Who do you think you are?" an internal voice may tell us, "Someone special? You've got it so good—why can't you appreciate the way things are? Why are you so selfish, always having *your way?*"

We feel bad, uncomfortable, whenever we try to move beyond the barrier that guilt has erected. And to avoid feeling uncomfortable, we simply remain within the confines of our self-made prison.

How can we break out of the guilt trap?

Consider this: If guilt is anger directed inward, couldn't that same anger become the energy for change?

*Yes!* It can.

The same energy that is predisposed to making us "feel bad" (blame ourselves for perceived "wrongs") can be redirected from *blame* to *change*, from a position of weakness (in some cases paralysis) toward a position of strength to change our *actions* or our *beliefs* about those actions.

Karen is a childhood classmate of mine who has had a great deal of pain to overcome. Shy and sensitive, artistic and musical, she grew up in a family of high achievers, black-and-white-thinking perfectionists. Her older brother was on his way to becoming a doctor; her sister, a science teacher. In high school, when Karen decided she wanted to become an artist, they (and her parents) ridiculed her "fluff" classes. When she announced she had enrolled in a beginning concert band class, they scoffed. She dropped the class. The same thing happened with drama.

She reasoned that their view of the world must be right, so she loaded up on science and math and literature—the "solids" that would "get her somewhere in life." Intellectually, Karen could well have handled the classes. Emotionally, she felt a sense of the "soul famine" we discussed in chapter three. So she halfheartedly attempted to keep her GPA up to her family's standards.

But Karen's heart wasn't in it. Her grades dropped and so did her self-esteem. She saw herself as "dumb" compared to her brother and sister. What was the use of trying?

As so often happens, Karen found a group of friends who accepted her just the way she was. Unfortunately, her new friends were into drugs and alcohol, life in the "fast lane." Karen eventually dropped out of high school, got pregnant, and married.

Karen and her young husband struggled for the first few years but eventually got their lives in order. He found work as a trucker, and Karen opened a day care center in their home.

Twenty-five years later, Karen's children are out of the nest. Her husband, still a trucker, is on the road a great deal of the time. It's time for Karen to live those long-ago cherished dreams.

What do you think is stopping her? Her barriers are many, but *guilt* is the primary culprit.

When I saw Karen not long ago we spoke about her dream of becoming an artist.

"Why don't you take your high school equivalency test?" I asked gently as we discussed her options (she had talked of her desire to attend a local community college). I knew she was bright; she could pass with flying colors.

Karen looked sad, defeated. "Why should I try doing something I failed at years ago? Besides, I'm not sure it's worth doing. All I want to do is *just* take some art classes."

She said "*it's*" not worth it, but I knew she meant *she* wasn't worth it, her personal dream wasn't worth it. She was *just* going to take some art classes, not lift her sights and follow her cherished dream. The value judgments of those she grew up with became incorporated into Karen's self-judgment of guilt.

How can we get beyond guilt's self-limiting belief system (one that brings with it a feeling of unworthiness, which we will get to in the following section)?

Changing deep-seated self-judgment that is guilt-based can take years. Sometimes work with a professional therapist is necessary. But for our purposes, let's consider some steps toward freedom from guilt.

1. In your journal, write the heading, "Guilt = Energy for Change."

2. Next, think about the goals (both general and long-term) you have for your life. Don't think about specific wants, desires, and dreams at this point. That will come later. Simply think about general goals such as "fulfillment for myself," "financial security as I age," "getting to know myself better."

3. Write down your goal or goals.

4. Now think about why you would judge any of these goals as being wrong, selfish, self-serving. Record your reasoning.

5. Think about why you would judge any of these goals as being right. Keep in mind chapter three's discussion on how you are intricately made by a wise and all-powerful God who does all things well. Record your reasoning.

6. Ask God to help you change your guilt belief and actions related to self-judgment. Specifically ask him to help you change the guilt actions that go against your primary goals.

7. Realize that you will not see change in this part of your emotional makeup all at once. But thank God for helping you with each step toward a healthier viewpoint, a healthier you.

8. Ask God to help you overcome any perfectionism that dwells within you, the "ideal you" that you struggle to compete with. Realize that this ideal is an idol that in reality doesn't exist. The real you is living, breathing, wonderfully made, wonderfully human, made to make mistakes and learn from those mistakes.

## Unworthiness

> It is difficult to make a man miserable while he feels he is worthy of himself and claims kindred to the great God who made him.
>
> ABRAHAM LINCOLN

For the sake of our topic, let's paraphrase Lincoln in the negative: "It's easy to make a woman miserable when she feels unworthy of herself and feels she isn't good enough to belong to the God who made her."

*Unworthy* has a synonym: *Undeserving*. And both words are mired in the emotional muck of feelings that tell us that we're not good enough, that we're inadequate, or even that we are somehow fundamentally deficient to everyone else.

Unworthiness is an interesting emotion in that we don't like to admit it's there. We can admit fear. Or guilt. Or discomfort.

But unworthiness?

Inadequacy?

Nosiree!! Not us.

That's because fear, guilt, and discomfort are all things that we put on in layers, like clothing. But unworthiness resides at our core. We honestly believe what it tells us is true: We *are* inadequate. We *are* somehow "less than" everyone else.

And so we hide it deep inside so that no one else will know. (Though because of its very nature, we suspect they know anyway.)

This makes the feeling of unworthiness the most hideous, insidious resident of our comfort zone. It leaves us feeling that we will never have what we want—the dream we long for—because after all, we're undeserving anyway. Not only that, but we *deserve* that condemnation.

Eric Hoffer said, "Our greatest pretenses are built up not to hide the evil and ugly in us, but our emptiness. The hardest to hide is something that is not there." And we do hide it. In fact, we become very clever at it. We pretend we're happy and worthy, but deep down, we believe its lie about who we really are.

Unworthy feelings and all their relations (inadequate, undeserving, deficient, "less than") form the barriers that keep us within the confines of our comfort zone. And by now you may have figured out that, one by one, we are examining the barriers and, one by one, looking at how these negatives can be turned into positive energy for living our dreams. And now, you're probably guessing that even something as insidious as unworthiness can be used to further our dreams.

You've guessed right!

Let me illustrate. Say you've made a list of all the dreams you want to pursue. You decide to pursue them all: return to school, complete your teaching credential, and become a teacher. *And* get a master's from UCLA's school of writing. *And*, of course, write a novel. *And* get an MBA so that you can become a stockbroker (and know how to invest all the money from your other pursuits). *And* become a graphic artist. *And* travel to the Galapagos Islands for *National Geographic. And* . . . the list goes on. Are we worthy of *any* dream we may want to pursue? The answer is, of course, a resounding *yes!* Are we worthy of *every* dream we want to pursue? Hmmmm. This requires closer examination.

Life isn't long enough, nor are we filled with adequate energy, to pursue all our dreams. Any one of those listed above would be more than enough to fill the time and energy of one dreamer.

Unworthiness (actually seen more as *humility* in this context) can work for us in determining which dream to pursue, helping us in a positive way to determine which of our dreams fit into the category of our strengths and which fit into the category of our weaknesses.

For instance, I may decide it would be fun to become a linebacker for the Rams. A healthy sense of unworthiness will put up a stop sign telling me my physique is wrong, my gender is wrong, my lack of thirst for blood, sweat, and violence is wrong for this dream. (Not to mention my aversion to pain.)

I am not worthy of becoming a linebacker for the Rams.

There is nothing wrong with my sense of unworthiness in this case. It's simply an assessment tool.

This is extreme, but I think the point is clear: Unworthiness can help determine those goals and dreams that are the best fit for who we are. In the next chapter we will consider those unique gifts God has given us and how they will determine which dream we will choose to live. A healthy sense of unworthiness will help us eliminate those dreams that are wrong as well as help us determine which dream will be successful.

In your journal, write the heading, "I am worthy to dream dreams and live my dreams."

1. Under the heading, write the Lincoln quote, "It is difficult to make a man miserable while he feels he is worthy of himself and claims kindred to the great God who made him."

2. Reread Psalm 139, prayerfully, reverently. Reach out with your heart and "claim kindred" to the great God who made you. If you like, reread portions from chapter three about how you were formed, concentrating on your created uniqueness and created purpose.

3. List the reasons why you are worthy of dreaming. For example, "I am created by a God who does nothing halfway." "He has given me unique gifts to discover and use." Or, "God created me for a purpose; he is giving me this opportunity to discover what that purpose may be."

4. Bow your head and ask God to help you understand who you are in his eyes. If your self-worth has been wounded in the past, you may have a difficult time with this journal entry. Reread—or rewrite, if necessary—those verses from chapter two, page 44 (Isa. 43:4; etc.).

## Discouragement

> Discouragement is simply the despair of wounded self-love.
>
> François de Fénelon

I picture discouragement similar to the cloud of dust that follows Pigpen in Charles Schulz's "Peanuts" comic strip. Only the cloud that follows us is made of gloom and sadness. Once it manifests itself, it can become a permanent part of our thinking, especially when it comes to leaving our comfort zone.

Discouragement can take on many manifestations: dejection, melancholy, depression, hopelessness, despair, despondency, gloom. The list goes on, but let's stop here before we get any more depressed! The reasons for these feelings are many: Others let us down. We let ourselves down. Someone, or maybe more than one person, has hurt our feelings. We failed in other pursuits, why should this time be any different?

One of the symptoms of discouragement is that the person under its cloud sees everything in tones of gray.

"Pursue my dreams?" she may scoff. "I can't do that."

"And why not?" we ask.

"Why should I? I wouldn't be any happier than I am right now."

And she's probably right—unless she moves out from under the cloud.

John-Roger and Peter McWilliams in *Do It! Let's Get Off Our Buts* tell an interesting fact about training elephants. When they are young, baby elephants are chained to stakes driven deep into the ground. No matter how hard it tries, the little elephant can't pull itself loose. Soon the baby elephant becomes discouraged and gives up. It simply doesn't move from where it is tethered. As the elephant grows, the trainer actually uses lighter and lighter restraints. By the time the elephant is full grown, it is kept from moving by a thin rope attached to a stick barely anchored in the earth.

Discouragement for us is what the rope is for the elephant. It makes forward movement seem impossible. Yet, in reality, it's just a stick (or a cloud) masquerading as something solid, something insurmountable.

Look closely at the causes of your discouragement. Make sure that you are not bound by the chains of childhood experiences and heartaches that you as an adult have the power to overcome.

How can we turn discouragement into the energy for change? Take a look at the root word in dis*courage*ment. Think about the root causes of your discouragement: Hurt feelings? Past failures? If these are part of your emotional makeup, that means that you probably have some anger hidden inside as well. The deep hurt (which probably happened because you cared so much) and resulting anger can be channeled in a different direction. But it will take *courage*—and faith—to move beyond the pain toward something you can't yet see.

Speaking of courage, this leads us to another consideration . . . what about broken dreams?

You may have experienced the heartbreak of shattered lifetime dreams: a divorce, the death of a spouse or a child, or the loss of someone else dear to you.

There is no quick healing for the pain that has pierced your soul. Your heartache—as well as your dreams, those broken, those yet to live—is unique to you. The only healing balm can come from the One who best knows you and your circumstances.

Consider that the hope found in pursuing a new dream may open your soul to wholeness, even to long-forgotten joy. Tim Hansel writes, "You can't laugh if you don't feel. You can't know true joy unless you've cried."

Every moment of your life is in God's hands, and this book of dream discovery may have found its way to you *in his perfect timing.* Undoubtedly, it will be more painful, more difficult, more fearful, for you to dream than it is for others, but prayerfully consider opening the door of possibility that is before you. And as you do, place your hand in that of the One who loves you, and step through into a world you may have forgotten existed.

## Procrastination

This was going to be the most profound section in the book. Honest, it was. But I didn't quite get around to doing the research I had planned to do.

The library was closed the first time I dropped by, so I stopped by a secondhand bookstore instead. I got caught up in a great mystery. Decided to buy it. When I got up to the cash register to pay for it, Susie (the store owner) and I started talking about our recent warm weather. Then she mentioned a really great place to get iced cappuccinos. So, of course, I had to try it out. (I have a great weakness for iced cappuccinos.)

Susie was right. It was wonderful! And I was delighted to find little tables with umbrellas and chairs—just the right spot to enjoy my cappuccino and read a few pages of the new mystery.

Well, minutes turned to hours, and before I knew it, twilight had descended.

I checked my watch and hopped in my car. Back to the library, I decided. (After all, I had this *really great* idea to research for this book.) Then I noticed my car was nearly out of gas. (I prefer a gas station near my home, the opposite direction from the library, unfortunately.) So I drove to the gas station, filled up, and checked my watch again.

Well, I really wanted to watch MacNeil and Lehrer.

Maybe I should just plan to go to the library tomorrow.

That's what I'll do, I decided.

But then the following morning, the day was so beautiful I decided to . . .

Never put off till tomorrow what you can do the day after tomorrow.

MARK TWAIN

Seriously, have you ever considered procrastination has a positive side? I've got good news for all us procrastinators: While we "wait" to begin a project, we are building energy within ourselves. We are using the "waiting" time to plan (sometimes unconsciously) how we will pursue our venture. And most importantly, we are creating a window of time in which we are forced to work at peak performance. Many people work very successfully under this kind of pressure. You can too—as long as you meet your end deadline.

So, procrastinators, dream your dream and prepare to act on your dream. Let procrastination work *for* you, not against you.

One last word about the comfort zone (and our getting ready to leap from its confines).

## Who's in Charge?

On the previous pages we've discussed those barriers that keep us within our comfort zone. These "barriers" are elements of our personalities that have been with us for decades. They know us better than we know ourselves (which is a pretty scary thought) and, though mostly illogical, can seem perfectly logical to us. They "lie" to us and cause us to back away from our dreams.

As we have seen, however, each of these negative feelings can be turned into tools for growth.

*Fear* can work *for* us, giving us an extra burst of energy and a sharpening of our senses as we move into the uncharted territory of our dreams.

*Guilt*, the same energy that is predisposed to making us "feel bad," can be redirected from *blame* to *change*, from a position of weakness toward a position of strength.

*Unworthiness* can help us determine which of our dreams fit into the category of our strengths and which fit into the category of our weaknesses.

*Discouragement*: Our deep hurts (even our resulting hidden anger) can be redirected. But it will take *courage*—and faith—to move beyond the pain toward something we can't yet see.

*Procrastination* gives us time to build energy within and design our venture before we begin. It also provides a window of time in which we are forced to work at peak performance.

All of these emotions can be seen as limiting to growth or as instruments of change. It's up to us to take charge of them, use them as fuel for the journey ahead.

As an example, say you are backpacking in the wilderness. You, without knowing what is inside, complain and whine about the heaviness of your pack. You trudge onward and onward, bent low beneath its weight.

Then suddenly, you zip open the pack. You find food and water—fuel—to replenish the energy you're expending.

Now you're glad to carry the weight. You know you'll use what's inside later on down the road. For now, though, that weight which once seemed nearly unbearable is no lighter but now bearable.

It all has to do with attitude—perceptions—about the baggage we carry. (And believe me, we all carry some.)

It's time to turn those negative barriers that threaten to imprison you into stepping stones toward your cherished dreams.

Let's do it now!

> Life moves on, whether we act as
> cowards or heroes.
> Life has no other
> discipline to impose,
> if we would but realize it,
> than to accept life unquestioningly.

Everything we shut our eyes to,
everything we run away from,
everything we deny,
denigrate or despise,
serves to defeat us in the end.
What seems nasty, painful, evil,
can become a source of beauty, joy
 and strength,
if faced with an open mind.
Every moment is a golden one
for him who has the vision
to recognize it as such.

HENRY MILLER

## Crashing into Someone Else's Comfort Zone

Oops!

I almost forgot to tell you: As our comfort zones expand, the "discomfort" zones of others may loom larger than we ever before noticed. This can be true of our spouses, our adult children, and even our friends.

If they have seen us as permanently fitting into their lives a certain way, any change in us (even positive change) may cause resentment.

My friend Marilyn, after twenty-five years of marriage, two kids married and gone, one poised and ready to leap from the nest, life heavily into the "doing for others" mode, decided to return to college.

She carried a heavy schedule and, because she lived an hour's drive from school, two additional hours disappeared from her day.

Marilyn has a heart the size of the Grand Canyon and had nurtured her children and her husband accordingly. For twenty-five years she had packed lunches for the kids and her husband (who worked shift work). She had excelled at baking and cooking. She was there for homework help, volunteered in the kids' classrooms, even served nine years on the local school board (two of those years as president).

You can imagine the discomfort Marilyn's family felt when she was no longer available to them.

They weren't just upset. They were *angry.* Even the two who were now married and gone gave her a bad time when they phoned and she wasn't there. Her husband felt deprived that he no longer had a lunch bagged and waiting in the fridge or a hot dinner on the table. Even community members raised their eyebrows, not understanding why she no longer was committed to doing the hands-on work she had done before.

Marilyn had stepped out of her comfort zone and, in committing to her dream, upset the "comfort" of those around her.

I recently asked Marilyn to tell me how her family is getting along now. (It's been eight years since she started back to school. She has completed her bachelor's and her master's degree in counseling. But more about that part of her story later!)

"It was tough on them, no doubt about it," she said. "But it just took time for everyone to adjust. The kids accepted it sooner than Ed did." Then she laughed, a bit sadly, before she went on. "Ed and I had a number of confrontations before things smoothed out. His mother had always done *everything* for his father. He had gone from living at home right into a marriage where I did *everything* for him."

"How did he finally begin to understand?" I asked.

"I think the best part of our relationship is our communication. None of this 'silent treatment' that so many couples face. We just talked it out. It turned out that his true feelings had nothing to do with whether or not his meals were waiting for him." She paused, a look of loving concern on her face. "He was afraid that as my world expanded, I would leave him behind. He was afraid I wouldn't love him anymore."

"How did you convince him that this wouldn't happen?"

"Once I understood his feelings, I did my best to assure him of my love. I also had to be open with him about what it meant for me to pursue a lifelong dream. And that was scary. I had to trust him to not make light of it or to try to get me to postpone it."

I smiled. "But after twenty-five years, you must have had a pretty good idea about how he'd react."

"Yes," she said. "It was safer for me than it can be for others who don't have the same open communication."

Barbara, another friend of mine, pursued much the same dream. She also had been married for a quarter of a century, though to a staunch and silent man with whom she had little open communication.

Through the years, when Barbara mentioned her desire to return to school and complete her degree, Jim ridiculed her, telling her she'd only flunk out the same way she had when they'd met in their teens.

But still the dream burned inside. The same day Barbara's daughters left for college, she drove to a nearby private school with a special degree program for returning adults. She didn't tell Jim where she was going.

"I nearly cried when I handed the counselor my transcript. I could feel my face turning beet red," she later told me. "I was so embarrassed. I just knew the woman would point to the door and tell me it was no use."

"What did the counselor tell you?"

Barbara laughed. "I couldn't believe it. She started adding up my credits. I had completed more classes than I remembered! Then she devised a schedule for me so that I could finish my B.A. in just a year and a half!" Barbara was nearly jumping out of her chair in her excitement telling me about it.

Then I asked, "What did Jim say when you told him?"

Her demeanor changed and a sheepish look crossed her face. "I didn't tell him."

"What?" I hadn't heard this part of her story.

"I decided I would wait until I had completed my first semester. If I did well—got good grades—I'd tell him. If not . . ." Her voice broke off.

"How did you do it—financially, I mean?"

She smiled. "First of all, I had saved up some money from my work at the tea shop. And the school counselor told me about a grant I could get for the rest of my tuition. I arranged my class schedule to coincide with Jim's work schedule. For several months he had no idea."

I took a deep breath. I couldn't imagine the pressure Barbara must have felt.

Barbara learned, even before she began to pursue her dream, the boundaries of her husband's comfort zone. Though she moved forward with her dream, she almost gave it up for fear of upsetting the balance (or imbalance) of their relationship. But the dream was too strong to die, and Barbara, at great risk, gave it her all.

I don't advocate deception when considering the pursuit of dreams and the comfort zones of those close to us. But when the dream is healthy and good, and we finally find our way out of our own comfort zones only to be blocked by someone else's, we do need to tread gently (as in Marilyn's case) or circumvent it (as in Barbara's case).

But before we judge Barbara's methods, let's hear the rest of her story.

"What happened when you finally told Jim what you'd been up to?" I asked.

"You won't believe this," Barbara laughed. "I not only did well; I received an outstanding achievement award from the English department: student of the semester. One student was picked from each department and they had a reception for us in the student center."

I nodded, waiting for her to go on.

She grinned. "I invited Jim to come with me. I didn't tell him where."

I gasped. "That could have been dangerous. What if he got angry when he found out what you'd done?"

Barbara smiled again. "Our verbal communication may not be all it should be, but I knew how he'd react. I knew he'd be proud."

"And he was?" I asked.

"Yes," she said. "He was. Very."

Barbara graduated from the university last spring. Guess who was sitting in the first row of the audience? You guessed it. Jim.

Barbara's story reminds me of a chorus we sometimes sing in church:

> Got any rivers you think are uncrossable?
> Got any mountains you can't tunnel through?
> God specializes in things thought impossible.
> God specializes in things you can't do.

As you prepare to dream, keep in mind that those you love may resent you, misunderstand you, even be angry with you as you change the parameters of their own comfort zones. This may be the final barrier you have to overcome in the pursuit of your dream.

So begin now to open your channels of communication with your loved one—though keep in mind it's still too early to share your dream. (Not because it's a secret, but because it's sacred.)

Hold close that sacred dream.

Defy the barriers that have kept you from dreaming.

Prepare to dream.

Dare to dream.

To Whom It May Concern:

I am chronically human. If the following signs are observed, I am not emotionally disturbed or dying.

1. If you find me stumbling and falling, I may be trying something new—I am learning.
2. If you find me sad, I may have realized that I have been making the same mistakes again and again—I am exploring.
3. If you find me frightened, I may be in a new situation—I am reaching out.
4. If you find me crying, I may have failed—I am lonely.
5. If you find me very quiet, I may be planning—I am trying again. These are life signs of beings of my nature. If prolonged absence of the above indicators is observed, do not perform an autopsy without first providing an opportunity and invitation for life to emerge.[1]

### Reflections

> He reveals deep and hidden things;
> he knows what lies in darkness,
> and light dwells with him.
> I thank and praise you, O God of my fathers:
> You have given me wisdom and power,
> you have made known to me what we asked of you,
> you have made known to us the dream of the king.
>
> DANIEL 2:22–23

This week, through prayer, bring into God's light those barriers that may keep you from dreaming. Scrutinize them. Understand them. Ask God for his wisdom and power to help you turn each barrier into energy for change. Thank him for the tools that you now have working *for* you as you dream.

*Father, reveal to us those deep and hidden things that threaten to keep us within our comfort zones. Expand the place of our tents, and stretch our tent curtains wide!*

# 6

# Exploring Our Gifts and Discovering Our Purpose

*We have different gifts, according to the grace given us. If a man's gift is prophesying, let him use it in proportion to his faith. If it is serving, let him serve; if it is teaching, let him teach; if it is encouraging, let him encourage; if it is contributing to the needs of others, let him give generously; if it is leadership, let him govern diligently; if it is showing mercy, let him do it cheerfully.*

ROMANS 12:6–8

## Who Am I Anyway?

In chapter three we discussed how each of us is the genetic combination of one of about 400 of our mother's egg cells with one of 360 million of our father's sperm cells. *Each of us could have been any one of about 144 billion distinct human beings!* Yet God handpicked the genes that went into our making, lovingly creating us to be the one distinct human being we are today—unlike anyone else in the world. And he filled us with just the right combinations of love and laughter and intellect and music and art and compassion and curiosity and creativity—personality ingredients that make us who we are.

No doubt about it! We are complex creatures.

It's no wonder that the age-old question that has plagued philosophers and thinking people through the centuries is, "Who am I?"

Oswald Chambers says this about our complexities:

> Personality is that peculiar, incalculable thing that is meant when we speak of ourselves as distinct from everyone else. Our personality is always too big for us to grasp. An island in the sea may be but the top of a great mountain. Personality is like an island, we know nothing about the great depths underneath, consequently we cannot estimate ourselves.[1]

Chambers is right—our personalities may be too complex for us to completely grasp. Yet, just as an island can be the tip of a mountain, it can be seen, it can be known, and it can indicate the geological makeup of what lies beneath the surface of the sea. And we can take a look at what we know about our gifts and our personalities and know, at least in some portion, about those dreams and desires that lie beneath the surface of our consciousness.

Maybe it will help to take a closer look at our gifts, those personality traits God has given to each of us. From the following list, record in your journal those traits that fit most closely with your personality. (Be generous with yourself; your list should number at least ten personality traits.)

| | | |
|---|---|---|
| Animated | Dynamic | Deep and thoughtful |
| Analytical | Detail conscious | Goal-oriented |
| Mediates problems | Agreeable | Neat and tidy |
| Patient | Sense of humor | Curious |
| Charming | Makes friends easily | Sincere |
| Born leader | Not easily discouraged | Organized |
| Likes to be in charge | Musical | Self-sacrificing |
| Empathetic | Conscientious | Pays attention to detail |
| Independent | Serious and purposeful | |
| Loves people | Loves nature | Enthusiastic |
| Quiet | Witty | Joyful |
| Works well under pressure | Would rather be outdoors | Loving |
| | | Loyal |
| Tender | Talkative | Cheerful |
| Practical | Inspiring to others | Orderly |
| Business-minded | Self-sufficient | Faithful |
| Good listener | Easy to get along with | Compassionate |
| Excels in emergencies | Likes lists | Appreciative of beauty |
| | Prefers to remain in the background | Persistent |
| Likes to be "on stage" | | Instills confidence in others |
| | Has a servant's heart | |
| Exudes confidence | Adaptable | Spirited |
| Thrives on opposition | Prefers being alone | Energetic |
| | Enjoys interacting with people | Enjoys intellectual pursuits |
| Pragmatic | | |
| Artistic | | |

Of those personality traits that you have recorded, number them in order of their importance to you, number one being the trait that you see most strongly evidenced in yourself.

Next, write ten sentences in your journal beginning with the words "I have," "I like," "I am," and so on, completing each sentence with a personality trait. Use the first ten traits from your list, again numbering them in order of importance. Number one will be that trait that you see as the most important in your personality.

As an example, you may record the following sentences in your journal:

1. I am compassionate.
2. I have a servant's heart.
3. I like an intellectual challenge.
4. I enjoy interacting with people.
5. I am a born leader.
6. I like to be "on stage."
7. I am not easily discouraged.
8. I exude confidence.
9. I instill confidence in others.
10. I am energetic.

A few months ago, I had the opportunity of interviewing Terri Sanders, a dynamic woman who had successfully begun a program for homeless families in South Los Angeles. Terri, an Episcopal priest, is in her forties and, I was surprised to find, had begun her career in midlife.

As we sat across from each other in an Old Town Pasadena restaurant, I asked Terri how that came about: How did a housewife and mother suddenly decide to go into full-time ministry?

Terri smiled, her charm and openness immediately putting me at ease. "It wasn't an immediate decision, though it may have appeared that way to someone observing me from the outside," she said. "I had held the dream of ministry close to my heart for years. It was too sacred to share. I knew I simply needed to wait for God's perfect timing."

A look of sadness briefly crossed her face. "Of course, I didn't know that my dream would be born by tragedy. After Bill's car accident, I was devastated. It happened the same year my twin daughters left for college. My life changed drastically. For years all my activities had been centered around family. But now I suddenly had no family, no activities. Nothing. Just a great, dark emptiness.

"At first I was angry at God for my loneliness, for taking Bill away from me. It took me a while to work through all of that. My faith helped. But because of my personality, I knew I needed to do something externally. I am an active person. I needed to actively move out of the internal—the grieving and sorrowful mode I was in—and do something external, something for someone else. Of course it took months to come to this place in the healing process."

Terri paused as the server set our salads on the table. As she stirred her coffee, she began to speak again, her voice still sad. "In the shock of my grief, I had completely forgotten my dream. Then one day as I was driving downtown, I saw a man with a sign that said, 'Will work for food.' Beside him sat a pregnant wife and a child about two years old. The hopeless looks on their faces reawakened something inside me I had forgotten about: my desire to help others, to minister, to dedicate my life to really making a difference in lives of children and families.

"And I wanted to do more than simply hand a homeless family money for food or even try to find temporary shelter. I had a dream of doing something that would make a complete difference—get the family off the street into a real home, with real jobs, tutoring for the children—a multifaceted effort.

"I'm pragmatic, even methodical, in my approach to most things." Terri laughed. "Even in my approach to pursuing a lifelong dream."

"What did you do first?" I asked.

"I began pouring my energies into exploring my options and analyzing the best approach to achieving my purpose, which was to help people."

"You set immediate goals?"

Terri nodded. "One of my dreams was to go to seminary. I wanted the intellectual challenge, and I knew that I needed the theological, psychological, and social background to achieve my purpose. So the first thing I did was enroll in Fuller Seminary.

"I completed my Master's of Divinity and was ordained into the Episcopal Church. And God opened the door for me to take a pastorate in South L.A. For the past four years I have been on the staff there."

"Tell me about your ministry to the homeless."

When she answered, I could tell by her expression that this was her passion, her fulfillment, her realization of a dream for herself, and for others.

"I have begun a training program for churches to 'adopt' homeless families. I travel to these churches, meet with the volunteers who've indicated interest, and help them begin the program. They work with one family at first, then can add more if they've got the resources. The volunteers collect money to pay for the homeless family's first and last month's rent in a clean and safe apartment. The volunteers collect furniture and cooking utensils, food supplies, and clothing. Someone volunteers to help with job training and job hunting skills. Someone else may volunteer to tutor the children so that they can catch up with their classmates. (Most homeless kids have had to drop out of school.) Psychological counseling sometimes is part of the intervention.

"We simply try to invest as much time and effort as possible in a program that will help the family get a healthy 'boost' to get off the streets and *stay* off the streets."

"You have achieved your dream?" I asked.

Terri folded her napkin and put it on the table. "The best part about this dream is that it keeps growing. There is some fulfillment with each new church that comes into the program, with each family that is able to get off the streets. But my dream never stays the same—it seems to stretch right along with the program." She smiled softly. "That's the best kind of dream to have."

You may have guessed by now that the sample personality "profile" we mentioned earlier is one that very easily would fit Terri's personality. She is compassionate (as we saw by her concern for the homeless), has a servant's heart (she wanted to do something to help), likes an intellectual challenge (she returned to graduate school—seminary), enjoys interacting with people (as evidenced by her desire to work with volunteers), is a born leader (she designed and began the homeless program), likes to be "on stage" (as evidenced by her teaching the volunteers at the volunteer churches), is not easily discouraged (she didn't give up after her husband died, even in her anger, loneliness, and sorrow), exudes and instills confidence (as evidenced in her ability to inspire and motivate others), and is energetic (as evidenced in what she has accomplished in just four years).

Terri's dream perfectly matched those "gifts" that God had placed within her personality.

Now let's take a look at a completely different personality type.

Mary Lou is my hairstylist and friend. Anyone first meeting Mary Lou would be impressed by her high level of energy and intelligence. She is tan, fit, and delicately pretty. You would never guess that she is the mother of four grown boys and the grandmother of four.

Because Mary Lou has pursued a very unique dream (more about this in a moment), I asked her to complete the profile of her personality strengths. She cheerfully agreed, and this is what she came up with:

1. I enjoy interacting with people.
2. I love nature.
3. I would rather be outdoors.

4. I am energetic.
5. I am business-minded.
6. I am goal-oriented.
7. I am organized.
8. I am serious and purposeful.
9. I am analytical.
10. I am detail conscious.

Mary Lou breeds Arabian horses. Because her business is small and risky (she keeps ten to twelve Arabians at any given time), she continues working as a hairstylist a couple of days a week. "This way at least I can buy their feed during the lean times," she's told me wryly more than once.

I had known Mary Lou just a short time when I asked her about the pictures of horses (right next to her grandchildren's photos) at her shop. Her pride was immediately evident as she began to tell me the story of her dream pursuit.

"When I was a little girl I wanted a horse, like so many kids do." She worked on my hair as she talked. "I never got one, but I never forgot my dream. I just knew that someday I would have a horse. Any horse." She laughed. "I didn't even know what an Arabian was when I was a kid.

"My dream remained in the back of my mind until I reached my thirty-ninth birthday. All at once I thought, *If I'm going to do this thing, I'd better get busy.* I made a promise to myself that I would buy my first horse by the time I reached my fortieth birthday." She grinned in the mirror at me as she paused from snipping around my neckline.

"What a way to celebrate midlife!" I said.

She nodded. "I had shared my dream with Tony, my husband, so when I began talking about its reality, he wasn't surprised."

"Did he support your dream?"

"Oh, yes. He was wonderful! He knew how much it meant to me, so he helped with all the preliminary work—such as figuring out how much acreage we would need. We began looking for horse property. Tony's in construction, so when we finally found the property we wanted, he was able to help design and build a barn.

"Then I started doing research—reading everything I could find on horses at the library. That was when I decided to buy an Arabian. It helped that our new neighbor was raising Arabians. She took me under her wing; I learned a great deal from her. She introduced me to other breeders. Helped me find just the right mare."

"She became your mentor."

Mary Lou nodded. "More than that. She became a good friend and honest advisor. When I wanted to settle on a less-expensive mare just for riding, she talked me out of it. She guessed correctly that with my love for horses, I might someday want to breed them. She said that a greater investment in the beginning would pay off in the long term. I took her advice. And she was right."

Mary Lou went on to tell me how her business has grown over the past ten years. What began as a hobby quickly turned into a serious business. Some of her finer young horses are being boarded and trained at various breeders throughout the western United States. Mary Lou's days are spent cleaning out the barn, exercising and riding various of her Arabians, and working out with a local trainer to learn better techniques for training her horses.

What an inspiration! All Mary Lou's dreaming and living of her dreams occurred after midlife! Her four boys were married and gone. But did Mary Lou settle back and take life easy? (She could have. At the time she bought her first Arabian, she owned her own hair salon, which was doing a brisk and successful business.) No. Instead, Mary Lou chose a courageous dream, a dream that has made a difference in her life.

"How has your dream changed your life?" I asked her not long ago.

Her face lit up as she answered. "It has completely changed the way I see the aging process. I feel younger than I did fifteen years ago, and it has to do with the wonder I feel. I still get excited over the birth of a foal or from watching one of my colts scamper beside his mother in the morning sunlight. And the breeding is exciting—waiting to see just how the genes will line up to produce what I hope will be the perfect horse."

Mary Lou looked serious for a moment. "I can't imagine how empty my life would be right now if I hadn't pursued my dream."

Think for a moment about Mary Lou's personality profile. She enjoys interacting with people (as evidenced in her interaction with other breeders and trainers); she loves nature (she loves her Arabians); she would rather be outdoors (as evidenced in her riding and the training workouts); she is energetic (how could she *not* be with all she does); she is business-minded (she turned a one-horse hobby into a multi-horse breeding business); she is goal-oriented (she never gave up her dream); she is organized (as evidenced by the care and feeding of her brood); she is serious and purposeful (as evidenced by her hobby quickly turning into a serious—though passionate—business); she is analytical (as evidenced by her research and continual analysis of Arabian genetics for breeding purposes); she is detail conscious (as evidenced by her careful attention to every detail of her business—from which colt would best work with which trainer to the number of workouts per horse per day).

Abraham Maslow said, "A musician must make music, an artist must paint, a poet must write, if he is to be ultimately at peace with himself." Add to that, a humanitarian (such as Terri), must reach out with mercy and joy to make a difference in her world if she is to be ultimately at peace with herself; and a lover of nature, a horsewoman (such as Mary Lou), must breed, train, and ride horses—experiencing the wind in her hair, the sun on her shoulders—if she is to be ultimately at peace with herself.

Reread the personality assessment profile you just completed in your journal. Prayerfully consider what it is that you must do—if you are to be at peace with yourself. Write your thoughts in your journal using this format:

Because I am a _____ I must _____ if I am ultimately to be at peace with myself.

If the first entry does not feel right, try another. Or another. Remember, there is no right and wrong here. You are not committing to anything. (Commitment to your dream will come later.) For now, this is simply an exercise to help you focus your dreams and align them with the desires of your heart.

After you have completed the above exercise, write in your journal the following verses from Psalm 37:3–5, 7.

> *Trust* in the LORD and do good;
>   dwell in the land and enjoy safe pasture.
> *Delight* yourself in the LORD
>   and he will give you the desires of your heart.
> *Commit* your way to the LORD;
>   trust in him and he will do this. . . .
> *Be still* before the LORD and wait patiently for him.

Underline those words in italics: <u>Trust</u>, <u>Delight</u>, <u>Commit</u>, and <u>Be still</u>.

Meditate on the above verses, prayerfully considering their meaning in your life as you prepare to dream. Record your thoughts in your journal.

Consider the following paraphrase:

Trust in the Lord's guidance as you prepare to dream;
Dream only those dreams that are worthy and good;
Dwell in the land of those dreams and enjoy safe pasture.
Delight yourself in the Lord and he will help you discover your heart's desire.

Commit your dreams to the Lord. Trust him with your
  dreams.
Be still before him in the silence of your heart,
Wait patiently for him to align your dreams with his purpose for you.


## What Is My Purpose?

If you have built castles in the air, your work need not be
lost; that is where they should be. Now put the foundations under them.

HENRY DAVID THOREAU

Helen Keller said, "Many persons have the wrong idea of
what constitutes true happiness. It is not attained through
self-gratification but through fidelity to a worthy purpose."

Determining our own "worthy purpose" may be the single
most important exercise in this book. It is our compass as we
begin our dream discovery. Our purpose will steer us clear
of dreams connected to financial gain, fame, or power that
could entrap us and keep our dreams empty.

But if we prayerfully consider that all we do as God's children—from the smallest detail of our lives to the largest—
can be done with the purpose of bringing glory to our God,
our dreams will take on a positive and meaningful perspective.

Before choosing our dream, we must first discover our
purpose. Some of us may become confused with the difference between goal and purpose. Let's take a look at their
definitions.

A goal is something tangible and achievable, something
we reach for that may be on our way to something else
(another goal). We can choose and achieve many goals.

Our purpose, however, is a direction that is fulfilled in each
moment we live, even while moving toward our goal. Oliver
Wendell Holmes said, "The greatest thing in this world is
not so much where we are, but in what direction we are mov-

ing." Our purpose determines our direction. We can set and achieve many goals, but our purpose remains set for life. In the nineteenth century, Mary Wollstonecraft Shelley said "Nothing contributes so much to tranquilizing the mind as a steady purpose—a point on which the soul may fix its intellectual eye."

Our purpose is God-given and is closely connected to who we are, to those personality traits we explored earlier in this chapter. (More about this in a moment.)

If we misunderstand our purpose (thinking that it is something to achieve) or misunderstand our goals (thinking that they are a direction) we may have trouble reaching our goals or living with purpose.

As we define dreams in this book, we are referring to goals, usually significant goals that in a profound way will fulfill our purpose. And as we define our "living of dreams," we refer to a life of movement from dream to dream—always with a purpose.

Let's explore ways to define our individual purpose. We will again be working with the list of personality traits from the previous section plus another list of actions to define ourselves. Please open your journal and write down those positive things you like doing the most. Use the following list, or if you like, add those of your own.

Giving
Sharing
Exploring
Teaching
Learning
Nurturing
Creating

Have fun with this exercise. Close your eyes. Picture scenes from your life—those experiences that brought you great satisfaction, joy, or fulfillment. What positive actions do you see yourself performing? If you are having trouble, ask God to help you bring to mind those qualities and actions that best define who you are.

Next, refer to those ten sentences you recorded from our earlier exercise in which you defined your personality traits. Pick one or two qualities that define you the most succinctly.

Create a sentence beginning with "I am," then add the personality trait (or traits) to the action you just defined. You may want to experiment with several before you settle on one. Your sentence—which will be your purpose—should be pithy and to the point. Here are a few examples:

If you chose "compassionate" and "conscientious" as your personality traits and "teaching" from the above action list, your purpose sentence would then read, "I am a compassionate and conscientious teacher." If you chose "dynamic" and "animated" from the earlier list and "exploring" from the action list, your purpose sentence would read, "I am a dynamic and animated explorer." Let's try another: If you chose "deep and thoughtful" as your personality traits and "learning" from the action category, your purpose sentence would be "I am a deep and thoughtful learner." And so on.

A word here to further clarify the difference between purpose and goals: If your purpose statement reads, "I am a compassionate and conscientious teacher," your goals might include returning to college to complete your degree, finding a teaching position, perhaps moving from elementary to secondary education, or even university level teaching. Even after you have achieved those goals/dreams, your purpose continues.

If your purpose statement reads, "I am a dynamic and animated explorer," your goals may include a return to school to train in a travel-related field, perhaps travel writing, finding a position with a travel or tour company, or perhaps moving into the field of freelance travel writing. If your purpose statement reads, "I am a compassionate and artistic explorer," your goals might then include a degree in photojournalism and the pursuit of a career working for an international humanitarian agency. Again, after you have achieved your goals/dreams, your purpose continues.

Or if your purpose statement reads "I am a deep and thoughtful learner," your goals might include returning to school to explore a career in a research-related field. (This is where your personality traits statements will help you determine your field.) Another goal might be to work with other researchers in your chosen field, exchanging and publishing your findings. Once again, even after achieving those goals/dreams, your purpose lives on.

But back to the exercise at hand. The right combination of qualities and actions may not be immediately evident, but if you will play around with the idea a bit, something will finally "click." You'll feel an inside sigh, an "*Aha!* This is it." You may feel a joy of recognition as well as a satisfaction of realizing that your life has had a direction all along.

As I have said earlier in this book, your dreams—and in this case, your purpose—belong to you alone. It's not that they are secret. They are sacred. Consider them apple tree seedlings growing in a nursery. You are the gardener who tends them, nurtures them, feeds, weeds, and fertilizes them. Someday others will see them when they are grown. They may enjoy the fruit from the boughs of your healthy, growing trees. Then others will understand the purpose. But until then, keep them deep within yourself.

Write your purpose statement in your journal in bold letters. Underline it. Place exclamation points after it.

This is who you are!

This is who your God made you to be.

Record your feelings about your purpose. Write with a sense of celebration! Write as if speaking to God about how he has made you.

Thank him for those gifts, those qualities that make up who you are.

Ask him to continue leading you toward his purpose for you.

The great French Marshall Lyautey once asked his gardener to plant a tree. The gardener objected that the tree was slow growing and would not reach maturity for one hundred years. The Marshall replied, "In that case, there is not time to lose; plant it this afternoon!"

JOHN F. KENNEDY

### Reflections

May the favor of the LORD our God rest upon us;
    establish the work of our hands for us—
    yes, establish the work of our hands.

PSALM 90:17

This week, review those pages in your journal on which you have written your qualities and statement of purpose. Reread Psalm 37:3–7, committing to memory the meaning of "Trust, Delight, Commit, and Be still" in your life. Celebrate those qualities God has placed within you. Eagerly anticipate the discovery of your dream.

*Dear Lord, we trust you with our dreams. We delight in who you've made us to be. We commit our way unto you. And we quiet ourselves before you, to commune with you, to seek your guidance.*

# 7

# Choosing a Dream

*Saddle your dreams
afore you ride 'em.*

MARY WEBB

In chapter one I quoted Dr. Robert Schuller, "What would you attempt if you knew you could not fail?" This question provides the foundation for this chapter. Please copy the question in your journal under the heading "Choosing My Dream." (Keep your journal open: More exercises follow. This is going to be a "working" chapter!)

To answer Schuller's question, we will need to spend time in thoughtful reflection and prayer. Before we move on, quiet yourself before God and ask him to help you choose your dream wisely.

Take a few moments to reflect on all he has done for you
in the past. Thank him for being with you, for blessing you,
and for providing for your needs.

Picture specific times in your life when you felt his intervention, his presence, his loving care for you.

In your journal, write down the blessings that come to
mind. Understand that we all seem to sense his intervention
after the fact. We look back and say, "Oh, yes. I see it now.
He was there all along."

Understand that he is with you now, a very real presence
and force in your life.

God will help you on your new journey.

He is *for* you as you dream.

Thank him for his presence and power in your life.

Write a personal paraphrase of Romans 8:31 in your journal: "If God is for me, who can be against me?"

In the previous chapters, we have examined our value (who
we are in God's sight); our need to nurture ourselves (physically, emotionally, intellectually, and spiritually); our comfort zone limitations (getting past the barriers of fear, guilt,
unworthiness, and discouragement); our gifts and purpose
(providing the framework for our dreams).

And now, finally, here it is! It's time to choose your dream.

You will be creating three separate lists in your journal:

*Part 1: Desires*
*Part 2: Desires + Abilities*
*Part 3: Desires + Limitations*

Take a deep breath, whisper a prayer, and pick up your
pen.

(Oh, first hang out a Do Not Disturb sign. Plan to spend
at least an hour working on this exercise.)

### Part 1: Desires
Write the heading, then under it list those things you want
that may or may not tie in with your dream. Have fun with

this. Free associate. Let yourself go. But keep your desires or "wants" worthy of your dream, worthy of you: This is not to be a want list having to do with greed, power, or fame. (Please no "I-want-a-new-red-sports-car" wants!)

A quick definition of "needs" and "wants" may be in order before you begin the exercise. *Needs* are those things you can't live without for even a short period of time: air, water, food, shelter, clothing, and protection. Everything else is a *want*.

For instance, your "want" list may include: "I want to travel," or, "I want to return to school," or, "I want to move to New Mexico," or "I want to learn a foreign language," or "I want to write a novel," or "I want to oil paint."

### Part 2: Desires + Abilities

After you are through listing your wants, choose the five most important. Leaving plenty of space to list your "abilities" under each "want," rewrite them under a new heading: Part 2: Desires + Abilities.

For example, if your "want" sentence reads: "I want to write and publish a murder mystery," leave space to also write your abilities, such as:

"I'm a good storyteller."

"I have a degree in English Literature."

"I know how to type."

"I have a devious mind."

And so on.

As you can see, you need to match your abilities and/or qualifications with each listed "desire" or "want." Again, have fun. Free associate. Write anything and everything you can think of. These abilities can include talents and training and personality traits from chapter six.

You may come up with abilities such as "I am adventurous," or "I'm a quick study," or "I'm artistic," or "I'm talented musically," or "I'm good with people," "I am persistent," or "I am creative." Let your imagination go. You are writing about *you*—a wonderfully complex, experienced, and gifted child of God. Don't be modest. Celebrate who you are as you work on this exercise. Your dream qualifications may be greater than you know!

### Part 3: Desires + Limitations

Rewrite your "want" list under this new heading. Again, leave plenty of space under each "I want" sentence to accommodate your "limitations" list. As we did in Part 2, write each of your top five "wants," followed by a list of liabilities relating to that "desire." Your list may look something like this:

"I want to write and publish a murder mystery."
(limitations) "I don't know a publisher."
"It would take too long to learn how to write a book."
"I couldn't handle getting rejection slips in the mail."
"I can't afford to buy a computer."
And so on.

Continue the exercise, writing down the remainder of your "want" list. Record your limitations with honesty. They may have to do with the barriers to dreaming (fear, guilt, unworthiness, and discouragement) that we discussed in chapter five. Write them and analyze and identify each for what it is.

When you have completed this list of limitations, take a moment to review it. What you perceive to be a limitation may not be.

Remember how we found that our barriers can work for us? Limitations can also be turned into advantages. Examine each limitation and see if you can find a positive use for it.

For example, take a look at the limitation: "I couldn't handle getting rejection slips in the mail." This limitation is based on fear, specifically fear of rejection. This fear is also based on the unknown. (In reality, you do not know whether or not rejection slips will come in the mail.) Remember: Fear can be the energizing force to move you beyond your fears. As I said in chapter five: In a new situation, all our senses need to be fine-tuned, in prime condition to bring to us all the information we need. This is exactly what happens when our bodies kick into a fear mode. Our sharpened senses, sensitivity, and heightened awareness (all begotten of fear) help us process the information more quickly and efficiently (pp. 93–94).

How will this fear work to help us move beyond a fear of receiving rejection slips in the mail? It will help us write a better murder mystery. It will motivate us to write the very best book we can to avoid receiving those little green slips.

Closely examine the limitation: "I can't afford to buy a computer." This is an excuse, not a limitation. Many books have been written on yellow legal pads with a pen or pencil. (John Grisham wrote his first novel this way—during long hours in court, I might add.)

As you work through this list, don't let barriers and excuses masquerade as true limitations. A true limitation would be a response to a want such as:

"I want to be an opera singer."

(limitation) "I can't sing."

Now that's a limitation!

In your analysis of limitations, look for a positive use for each. Write that *positive attribute* next to it—in bold lettering. Next to the excuses, write "excuse," also in bold. If you perceive your limitation to be real, leave it for now.

Your limitations list may now look like this:

(limitations) "I don't know a publisher." EXCUSE: THERE ARE LISTS IN THE LIBRARY.

"It would take too long to learn how to write a book." IMPATIENCE: I WILL BE IMPATIENT FOR SUCCESS.

"I couldn't handle getting rejection slips in the mail." FEAR: I WILL WRITE THE BEST BOOK POSSIBLE TO AVOID THEM.

"I can't afford to buy a computer." EXCUSE: I CAN USE A TYPEWRITER OR PAD AND PENCIL.

Take time with this exercise. Be creative. (It's a worthwhile exercise for most of life's limitations.)

## Comparing Abilities and Limitations

The next step in this exercise is to cross-compare Part 2: Desires + Abilities with Part 3: Desires + Limitations.

Take a few minutes to page back to Part 2 in your journal. Prayerfully consider your five listed "wants" with your abilities listed beneath them. As you analyze each, flip forward to the same "want" listed in Part 3, taking a close look at the limitations listed.

How do they compare? When combined, your list may now appear like this:

"I want to complete my graduate degree."

(abilities) "I graduated from college with a 3.5 GPA."

"There is a university in my hometown offering graduate degrees."

"I am goal-oriented."

(limitations) "I graduated from college more than twenty-five years ago!" FEAR: I WILL USE MY FEAR TO WORK HARDER.

"The university is private. I can't afford the tuition." DISCOURAGEMENT: I WILL TURN IT INTO *COURAGE* AND INVESTIGATE SCHOLARSHIPS, GRANTS, OR PURSUE A DEGREE FROM A PUBLIC UNIVERSITY.

## Narrowing the Field of Dreams

After you have analyzed both lists, seriously considering both the positives and negatives of each, choose the "wants" that:

1. Create in you the greatest passion when considering their pursuit.

2. Have the greatest numbers of listed "abilities."

3. Have the least numbers of *real* "limitations."

Write the chosen "desires" in your journal, listing after each its "abilities" and "limitations." (You may have narrowed the field to one or two or you may have several listed.)

By now, I hope you have memorized your purpose statement. Write it from memory near your "wants." (If not, peek back a few pages to chapter six's journal exercises.)

Compare your purpose statement with your "I want" statements. How does each fit into your purpose? (Remember, our goal is something tangible and achievable, something we reach for on our way to another goal. Our purpose is a direction that is fulfilled in each moment we live, even while moving toward our goal.) Your "want," if it becomes your goal, must fit into your purpose.

Let's consider one of our earlier examples from the "I want" exercise. (We'll call our would-be mystery writer "Sue," to avoid confusion later on.) Sue writes:

"I want to write a murder mystery."

(abilities) "I'm a good storyteller."

"I have a degree in English Literature."

"I know how to type."

"I have a devious mind."

(limitations) "I don't know a publisher." EXCUSE: THERE ARE LISTS IN THE LIBRARY.

"It would take too long to learn how to write a book." IMPATIENCE: I WILL BE IMPATIENT FOR SUCCESS.

"I couldn't handle getting rejection slips in the mail." FEAR: I WILL WRITE THE BEST BOOK POSSIBLE TO AVOID THEM.

"I can't afford to buy a computer." EXCUSE: I CAN USE A TYPEWRITER OR PAD AND PENCIL.

Sue then compares her purpose statement to what she has written: "I am an artistic, spirited creator." It fits beautifully!

But what if Sue's purpose statement were this: "I am a deep and thoughtful nurturer." Does her "I want" fit? It might work, but probably not. Because her goal of writing a mystery novel would not fulfill her need to nurture, she might find herself growing frustrated with the solitary writing process.

Let's take a look at another example. We'll call our would-be graduate student "Jan" and compare her "I want" list with her purpose statement:

Jan wrote: "I want to complete my graduate degree."

(abilities) "I graduated from college with a 3.5 GPA."

"There is a university in my hometown offering graduate degrees."

"I am goal-oriented."

(limitations) "I graduated from college more than twenty-five years ago!" FEAR: I WILL USE MY FEAR TO WORK HARDER.

"The university is private. I can't afford the tuition." DISCOURAGEMENT: I WILL TURN IT INTO *COURAGE* AND INVESTIGATE SCHOLARSHIPS, GRANTS, OR PURSUE A DEGREE FROM A PUBLIC UNIVERSITY.

Let's suppose Jan's purpose statement reads like this: "I am a deep and thoughtful learner," or "I am a practical and patient teacher." The first is, of course, a perfect fit. The second also fits with her want statement, "I want to complete my graduate degree," but it may indicate that this dream, this goal, is the first of many leading to a bigger dream, that of teaching. (More on this bigger dream in a moment.)

Continue comparing your "I want" list (that now includes your abilities and limitations) to your purpose statement. You will notice that some of your wants will naturally move into stronger positions—contenders for your big dream—as it becomes apparent that they fit into your purpose. Set aside those wants that don't fit. Underline the "I want" statements that fit into your purpose. Then stop for a moment.

*Stop?*

Yes. Stop.

This has been an intense exercise: It's time to take a break. (And besides, I want to tell you one of my favorite stories about one of my favorite people.)

So pour yourself a cup of tea, settle into a comfortable chair, put your feet up, and let me tell you about my friend Marihelen. (We'll get back to choosing our dream in a few minutes.)

## What about Impossible Dreams?

I was five years old the first time I saw Marihelen. My family had just moved into town. ("Town" was Big Creek, California, a small community of about one hundred families nestled among pines and granite cliffs deep in the Sierra Nevada mountain range.)

I had been standing in my new front yard alternately watching fuzzily-striped bees buzzing around the lawn's carpet of clover and staring at a sky bluer than I'd ever seen. I looked up to see a little girl, slightly older than myself, staring intently at me across the picket fence.

I stared back at the dark-haired, skinny-legged, unafraid-of-anything-looking child.

Her expression was at once friendly and challenging. "You're supposed to stomp those," she said, looking at the bees.

I shrugged, acting as if I knew that.

"Barefoot," she added.

I stared at her, figuring she was kidding. Her moss-colored eyes looked dead serious.

"Show me," I said.

She nonchalantly opened my gate and let herself into my yard.

"Get a jar," she commanded as she unstrapped her sandals. "Actually, get two. We'll see who can stomp the most."

I nodded, not daring to show my fright, and did as she bade.

In awe, I watched as she began to stomp bees, stunning them into inactivity, picking them up by their wings, and dropping them into her jar. There was a look of joyful abandon—even determination—on her sun-reddened face.

After a few minutes, she stopped and looked at me. She didn't say a word, but the challenge in her eyes was evident.

I took a deep breath and thought of nothing else but the unspoken dare: not the blue sky above me, the hissing of grasshoppers under the manzanitas, or the chattering of squirrels and Steller's jays in the towering pines. My mind was set to act: I knew this test would prove I was worthy—or unworthy—of her friendship.

I squatted in the grass and slowly unlaced my shoes, then pulled off my socks. I couldn't help noticing my bare feet looked white and tender compared to those of the tough little girl (she still hadn't told me her name) who stood beside me.

Then I stood and, biting my lip, went after my first bee.

I stomped down quick and hard on that bee; I figured I had the best chance if I moved faster than he could turn his little stinger upward to sting me. As an added caution, I stomped him again. And again. And again.

"Don't squash him," my new friend said. "You won't be able to pick him up by his wings if he's all squishy."

I looked at her and grinned. "I know that," I said with confidence, then began stomping another unsuspecting victim.

I don't remember when Marihelen finally told me her name. But from that day on we became inseparable. She was my hero, everything I wanted to be. (Older, for one thing; she was six and I was still five and a half.) She climbed trees faster and higher than any other kid in town; she told the scariest stories during outdoor sleep-overs; she knew just where the best frogs could be caught and always caught the most—bare-handed; she learned how to cook French toast covered with powdered sugar, all by herself, before she turned seven; she could imitate a monkey's face, looking cuter than the real thing; and she changed her name from Mary Helen to Marihelen because she hated it when teachers called her Mary.

Needless to say, I was in awe. I aspired to be just like Marihelen.

When she got her first pair of glasses in second grade, I couldn't wait until I got mine too. (Although I had to wait two years because no one listened when I said I couldn't see the chalkboard. My teachers and parents thought I just wanted to be like Marihelen.)

Then Marihelen began having trouble in school. (We were in the same first and second grade combination classroom, though I was still in first grade.)

I watched as my hero—my friend who could do everything better than everyone else—found something she couldn't do very well, maybe couldn't do at all: Read.

Marihelen couldn't learn to read.

At first it was thought to have something to do with her eyesight. She had a crossed eye. Her doctor recommended an eye patch, which she wore for awhile. It didn't help, so he recommended surgery.

But after her eye healed, Marihelen still couldn't read.

Mrs. Jacobs, our first and second grade teacher, was patient and kind. She worked with Marihelen, tried to teach her to read, then finally recommended that she spend an extra year in second grade. "Maybe she's just missed too much school because of surgery," she said kindly to Marihelen's parents. "The extra year in second grade will give her time to catch up."

Marihelen was devastated. Everyone would know she "flunked" a grade. I, being a selfish little creature, was secretly delighted. Now my friend and I could go through school together, grade by grade.

We moved into third grade together. Our teacher loved music and drama. Our class performed plays. We memorized poetry. We learned to play musical instruments and performed in the school auditorium. No one seemed to notice that Marihelen still had not learned to read.

Then came fourth grade. Our teacher, Mrs. DeMasters, had a different opinion about school. There was to be no more music, art, or plays. It was time to get serious about our studies.

Mrs. DeMasters—at best strict, and at worst mean-spirited—noticed that Marihelen couldn't read. She labeled my best friend lazy. And she informed the whole class of her opinion. After all, anyone who had the desire could learn to read. And if you didn't have the desire—well, obviously you were lazy. (In the fifties, no one had heard of dyslexia or any learning disabilities.)

Marihelen was made to stay after school to complete unfinished schoolwork or homework. I waited for her by the playground, agonizing with her as we walked home from school—with Marihelen barely able to hold back her tears, feeling worse about herself day by day.

Then along came Jeanie to the rescue, Marihelen's little sister, bright as a penny and smart as a tack. Jeanie, a year her junior, made E's (E for Excellent; precursor of A's) in all her subjects.

Jeanie, both kindhearted and enterprising (susceptible to bribery with extra cookies, desserts, and such), agreed to do Marihelen's homework.

*"Aha,"* said Mrs. DeMasters, when she saw the improvement in Marihelen's homework. "I knew you could do it if you just tried." Then, "See, class! This is what you can achieve if you just put your mind to it!"

And so it became a pattern—through fifth, sixth, seventh, and eighth grades—then into high school. Marihelen took the lightest-weight classes she could, mostly in the areas of art and homemaking. Year after year, Jeanie "helped" Marihelen with homework so that she could pass to the next grade.

In high school, Marihelen, as pretty and vivacious as ever, became active in student council, an easily elected officer each year. She was selected our class princess for the winter ball and our class sweetheart for the homecoming dance. Our final year in high school, she was voted "best liked" in the senior class.

We graduated.

Marihelen still had difficulty reading.

After attending twelve years of school together, Marihelen and I sadly parted company. I left for college in Southern California. Marihelen enrolled in a city college near our hometown. She declared an art major, took a few classes, then, not surprisingly, dropped out to marry.

Marihelen and her husband raised three lovely children. Marihelen, during her years of hands-on motherhood, actively participated in church and community affairs, particularly those having to do with her children's school. She volunteered in her children's classrooms, taught Sunday school, and—for six consecutive years—served on the local school board.

Her life was full of love and laughter and activity. Her home became a haven to her children's friends during their teens. She counseled and befriended them. Even their parents sought her wise counsel.

But there was something missing. Something incomplete in her life. Marihelen wanted to return to school.

She wanted to graduate from college, get her bachelor's degree, maybe go on for a master's.

*Marihelen*—who barely made it through high school? Go for advanced degrees? Talk about a seemingly impossible dream!

But it didn't seem impossible to Marihelen.

She held her dream sacred and close, for a long time telling no one what she someday planned to do.

Let's take a break from the story and examine Marihelen's want list:

"I want to return to school—complete my bachelor's degree, and possibly my master's degree."

(abilities) "I am determined."

"I am motivated."
"I am goal-oriented."
"I am conscientious."
"I understand the value of education."
(limitations) "I have difficulty reading."
"The nearest college is an hour way, across treacherous mountain roads."
"I have a history of academic failure."
Even if Marihelen added positive attributes to her limitations list, it would not change how heavily weighted her list is toward the negative. (The lesson here for us? Determination and motivation are worth tenfold their equivalents on the limitations list.)

Let's take a look at her purpose statement. (I think I can accurately create this for her because I know her so well.) "I am a patient and joyful learner and nurturer."

Does her dream fit her purpose? You bet it does! And, as you will see when we get back to the story, Marihelen's dream fits better as she continues to live it.

One day several years ago, Marihelen called to tell me that she had enrolled in city college. That first semester, she said, she planned to begin with just one class—remedial reading—and see if she could successfully complete it.

"Are you scared?" I asked, ever the tentative one.

Marihelen laughed. "Are you kidding? I'm scared spitless! But I'm going to do it. I'm going to succeed." Though we were on the phone, I knew by her tone the expression that was on her face. I was sure it was the same look of joyful determination she'd had during her sting-defying bee stomp some thirty-five years before.

Marihelen made it through her first class with aplomb. Through trial and error, she began to better understand her learning disability. She didn't let it stop her. She understood that she needed longer to read any given section in her assigned texts. She would read, reread, and test herself for understanding. She taped lectures and listened to them again and again.

Gradually she added more classes, though never over-loading herself so that she wouldn't have the extra time she required for studying.

She graduated from city college with her Associate of Arts degree, maintaining a solid 3.5 average.

She enrolled in a nearby state university and declared a liberal arts major. Class by class, usually carrying around nine units per semester, Marihelen lived her dream.

And then one sunny afternoon in May, two years ago, Marihelen, in cap and gown, marched down the aisle of the university's stadium to receive her B.A.

Marihelen, "patient and joyful learner and nurturer," had dared to dream an impossible dream.

Our dreams may be as impossible as my friend Marihelen's—or they may fit into a more attainable category. But they are as sacred and wonderful, as achievable, as hers.

Let's continue with our own journey of dream discovery.

When we left our journal exercise, you were comparing the "I want" list (that includes your abilities and limitations) to your purpose statement. And you had underlined the "I want" statements that most closely fit into your purpose.

Prayerfully and thoughtfully, consider the underlined wants now.

Next, close your eyes and visualize yourself as having successfully achieved some or all of your wants.

If it's returning to school, imagine yourself walking down the aisle and receiving your diploma. How does it feel? Examine your feelings.

If it's writing a book, imagine yourself holding your completed manuscript, or the published book, in your hand. How does it feel?

If it's starting a community theater group in your hometown, imagine opening night with the audience full and the performers taking a bow. How does it feel?

If it's going after your pilot's license, imagine completing your first cross-country flight—alone. How does it feel?

And so on.

You may do this visualization exercise with as many of your dreams as you wish. Let your imagination soar.

If any one of these dreams is going to be your big dream, you will be wearing it for a long time. It must fit. It must *feel* right. Take your time, and, as I've said with many of these exercises: Have fun.

After you have completed this, record those dreams that seem the best fit. A quick review of those items that constitute a worthy dream may help: These dreams should:

1. Create within you the greatest passion when considering their pursuit.
2. Have the greatest numbers of listed "abilities."
3. Have the smallest numbers of *real* "limitations."
4. Fit into your purpose statement.
5. "Feel" right when you "wear" them.

## Further Narrowing the Field of Dreams

How will we ever choose just one dream?

By now the field will have narrowed to just a few "wants" or dreams (as we will now call them). If you are still having trouble settling on just one, try reviewing your "wants" list to see how many of your wants fit into your final contenders. For instance: Perhaps one of your wants is to live in New Mexico. Another might be to travel. And another may be to paint with oils. Or sculpt. Or teach. But the big dream you are considering is that of completing a degree program. Some of your "lesser" wants will automatically fit into the bigger dream: "I want to return to school to complete my degree."

You may want to pursue a degree in art, move to New Mexico, paint and sculpt. A living dream might mean completing a teaching credential at a later time.

Or someone considering a big dream of becoming a mountain climber may find an automatic fit with wants such as wanting to travel, shoot photos, learn a foreign language, and so on.

Now for the tough part. It's time to eliminate all your wants except the one that is going to become your big dream. Be ruthless. You have only time for one pursuit.

Choose your dream.

One dream.

Try it on.

Wear it proudly.

Lift it up in praise to the God who gave it to you.

Celebrate it.

Write it on a fresh page, this time instead of beginning with "I want," however, begin with "I will" and complete your sentence:

"I will become a photojournalist."

"I will complete my degree."

"I will become a commercial artist."

"I will write and publish a book."

"I will teach children with special problems."

"I will get my Ph.D."

"I will climb Mt. Everest."

Your dream is ripe for dreaming. Your moment is ripe for acting.

Oswald Chambers has said, "Dreaming about a thing in order to do it properly is right; but dreaming about it when we should be doing it is wrong." Henry David Thoreau said, "If you have built castles in the air, your work need not be lost; that is where they should be. Now put the foundations under them."

Through this book we've been laying the foundations for your dreams. The bricks and fresh mortar are ready for you, the builder, to place in the proper order to create the structure of your very real, very attainable, achievable dream.

Dear dreamer, it's time to pick up the trowel and begin.

➤➤➤

### Reflections

> I will go before you
>     and will level the mountains;
> I will break down gates of bronze
>     and cut through bars of iron.
> I will give you the treasures of darkness,
>     riches stored in secret places,
>     so that you may know that I am the LORD,
>     the God of Israel, who summons you by name.
>
>                                         ISAIAH 45:2–3

This week, celebrate your dream. Know that it *will* happen—because you, with God's help—*will* act on your dream. You *will* live your dream. Your mighty God goes before you. Thank him for his presence.

*Father, thank you for revealing those treasures of hopes and dreams so long forgotten, so long hidden in the secret places. We praise you that we have no greater treasure than that of Jesus Christ dwelling in us.*

# 8

# Finding a Hero

*Have I ever told you
you're my hero?
You're everything
I would like to be.
I can climb higher
than an eagle.
You are the wind
beneath my wings.*

LARRY HENLEY
AND JEFF SILBAR

George Bernard Shaw once said, "The only service a friend can really render is to keep up your courage by holding up to you a mirror in which you can see a noble image of yourself."

Often as we begin our journey into uncharted territory, we need a hero, someone who has dreamed a dream as big as ours and has lived her dream. We need a friend to give us courage as we dream, to hold up a mirror in which we can see our noble image.

Three significant things are happening as we begin our journey:

1. The nest has emptied and we are more physically alone than we have been in years.

2. Our comfort zone has expanded and is continuing to stretch. When this happens, others may "move away" emotionally because we are upsetting their own comfort zones.

3. Pursuing dreams is an intimate journey of discovery. For that reason, there are few people with whom we may want to discuss the process, especially in the dream's earliest stages.

But we need to hear words of encouragement and testimonies of challenges overcome. We need to find someone who has begun a similar course and is pursuing it successfully.

Our mentor, or hero, should be a positive, action-oriented person, someone who is open to the exchange of ideas and freely gives affirmation. How do we go about finding such a person?

Many of us find our mentors after we have begun to actively pursue our dreams.

Judith found her mentor—actually more than one—after she started back to school at a local community college.

"I was astounded," she said, "to find so many other women my age and older. When I registered for classes I assumed I would be the only middle-aged woman wandering around campus.

"But when I sat down in my first class and looked around, I nearly fell out of my chair. On one side was an eighteen-year-old kid, on the other a woman in her seventies! The class was made up of people of all ages. In fact, some of the older students interacted with the instructor more than the younger students."

"That must have been a relief." I knew Judith had been

fearful to return to school. And she hadn't had any encouragement from her husband. She had begun her dream pursuit very much alone.

Judith laughed. "It was more than that. It turned out to be *wonderful!* After that first class, four women around my age asked me to join their study group. Beginning the next day, we met in the student center, grabbed cups of coffee, went over our lecture notes and studied together. I found out that a couple of them were in my algebra class and one was in my science class. We exchanged phone numbers and arranged to meet regularly. I learned a lot from them; most of them had been there a semester or two. But mostly they gave me encouragement, the impetus to keep going when things got rough.

"Their help was invaluable. I no longer felt so alone. We exchanged information on course requirements. It became an informal support group. We stayed in touch even after they left to complete their degrees at a local university."

Charlene found her mentor when she enrolled in an adult education class to pursue her dream of writing a children's book. The course was simply titled "Writing Fiction," and though it was a six-week course, it set into action events that would change Charlene's life.

She signed up for the course, excited but nervous. The first evening, Charlene peered around the classroom and became immediately intimidated by her fellow students: One young man set an entire manuscript on his desk with a hefty thud and settled into his chair with a bored "professional writer's" look on his face. A woman sat visiting with her neighbor throwing out phrases like "point-of-view character" and "maintaining tone" and "character's voice." Another middle-aged couple (brother and sister, she found out later) discussed the first draft of a historical novel they had just completed.

Charlene gulped and checked the distance to the door. She wished she hadn't seated herself so close to the front of the room. It would have been so much easier to slip out discreetly if she'd only had the foresight to sit in the rear of the room.

Then the instructor, a woman named Alyssa Sharpe, entered the room. Based on her description in the catalogue ("Published Author of Six Mysteries"), Charlene had expected someone resembling the matronly Jessica Fletcher of *Murder, She Wrote*. Instead, a tall woman, magnificently dressed in colorful ethnic clothing with wildly curling hair and large hoop earrings, seated herself on the desk at the front of the room. She smiled warmly at the class and asked the students to identify themselves and tell a bit about the writing they'd done.

Nearly everyone had published something or at least attempted to. Charlene felt her face flush when her turn to speak came.

"I'm just beginning," she managed. "I've always loved to write, but I've been so busy with my family—raising kids—that I haven't had much time for myself." She glanced around the room to see if anyone else could identify. Apparently they couldn't. "I—I want to begin writing children's stories. Um, fiction, I think."

"That's great," said Alyssa Sharpe, her voice holding a tone of encouragement. "Do you have any plot ideas?"

"Actually, I do. I've been doing some research on something that happened in the nineteenth century—a true event. I want to use that as the backdrop for my story."

"Then it sounds like you're ready to begin. For next week's class I want you to develop a synopsis of your story. Make up a main character, create her history and description— make her come alive in your mind and to the rest of us."

Alyssa went on to discuss assignments with the other students. "And make sure you bring photocopies of your work to hand out to the class. This is an interactive course. We will be critiquing each other."

During the following week, Charlene not only completed her assignment, she went a step beyond and began her first chapter. She poured her heart and soul into her story. The process was difficult, but she felt an energy well up inside that she had never imagined could come from writing.

She went back to class the following week and excitedly awaited her turn to read and be critiqued.

But as others read, Charlene realized how little she knew of the mechanics of writing. She realized in horror that her punctuation was incorrect and that her dialogue wasn't even in the right paragraph form.

Again, she could feel her cheeks flush and felt the urge to run out the door before it came time for her reading.

But it was too late. She heard the instructor call her name.

Charlene passed her manuscript photocopies to her classmates. "I've got a lot to learn from all of you," she said before she began to read. "I apologize—"

Alyssa Sharpe interrupted. "Don't ever apologize for your work, Charlene." She looked around the classroom. "Actually, this advice is for all of you. Your work is your own—uniquely yours. Writing is complex; there are the ideas, the tone, the story, the characters, a million other things to consider when you're writing. None of us can get it all right all at once. It's a process. And we all have to begin somewhere."

And then Charlene began to read, her voice a bit quavery but building with confidence as the time passed.

When she finished, the room was silent. For a long time no one spoke. *Oh, no,* she thought. *It must've been worse than I thought.*

Finally, the instructor spoke, her voice strangely subdued. "You don't have a children's book there, Charlene."

Charlene felt her cheeks suddenly flame. She guessed Alyssa's next words would be something like, "You might as well give up and go home."

But after another moment of silence, Alyssa said, "What you've got there is certainly not for children. You've got a story that can turn into a blockbuster of an *adult* novel."

There were murmurs of agreement from class members. All at once the other writers began commenting on her story, her style, her "voice," her "tone," her plot. They were critiquing her work—and it was positive! It was wonderful! Charlene felt ten feet tall.

A few weeks later, when the six-week course was drawing to a close, Alyssa asked if anyone was interested in continuing the class informally at her home once a week. Charlene was the first to sign up.

And she began the painstaking process of serious fiction writing. Others from the original class gradually fell away, usually giving up the writing process and going on to other things. New members joined. Some stayed for awhile. Some didn't.

But Charlene stayed on. For five and a half years she worked on her novel, growing and stretching as a writer, honing her craft, writing, rewriting, critiquing, being critiqued.

Faithfully she sought Alyssa's advice. And Alyssa, believing in Charlene's talent, encouraged her to keep going during the lonely writing process and not to give up during the publisher-or-agent-finding process.

I recently congratulated Charlene when I heard that her seven-hundred-page novel had been accepted for publication.

"It took you five-and-a-half years!" I exclaimed, "How did you keep the momentum going?"

Charlene smiled. "It wasn't easy. But it helped to have the support of other writers going through the same process—just being able to commiserate with each other about the hard work and the rejection that you feel when your manuscript is making the rounds to agents and publishers."

"How about Alyssa?" I asked, though I had already guessed the answer. "How much did her 'mentoring' help you?"

Charlene's eyes brightened. She slowly shook her head as if still in awe. "Early in our acquaintance, Alyssa told me something that most of her readers and fans don't know. She wrote her first book at the age of forty. She had been through a divorce and had left her home state to start a new life. She drove to California with only what she could fit into her car. Through gutsy determination, she wrote that first book, then found an agent to peddle it to publishers. And of course, after the first book did so well, the agent was eager to sell another. She's now produced six books.

"When I got discouraged, it was easy to be uplifted by someone who had felt the same kind of discouragement. Knowing she had found success after all her hard work helped too. She often said to me, 'Charlene, if I could do it—you can too.' And so back I would go to my rewrite, all the more determined to finish what I'd begun, to complete my dream. Knowing someone like Alyssa believed in me was the greatest carrot that could be dangled in front of my nose."

"Are you working on another book now?"

Charlene grinned. "Of course. And I'm still working in Alyssa's class."

"Why? You've achieved what you had intended—the expertise, the experience."

"You never outgrow the need for a mentor. Alyssa herself has belonged to a critique group, led by her mentor and friend, for the last eleven years." Charlene laughed quietly. "You won't believe this—she's trying to convince me it's time to begin a critique group in my home for new writers." She paused, looking a bit embarrassed. "Can you imagine me, who just a few years ago was scared to read aloud in class, leading a group of my own?"

"You said it best, Charlene," I said. "Other dreamers find that their greatest encouragement comes from those who

know firsthand what they're feeling, who know what they're
going through. I can't think of anyone else who could be a
greater encourager than you!"

Another dreamer found her mentor and friend at a church
retreat high in the pines of the San Bernardino mountains.
Maggie, a single mother, was relatively new to her church.
Because of countless hours spent caring for Jodi, her men-
tally handicapped child, Maggie had not had time to interact with other women in the church. When Maggie's mother
volunteered to watch Jodi for the weekend, with a grateful
heart Maggie accepted the invitation to the ladies' retreat.
She knew that this would give her the opportunity to refresh
herself in God's Word and perhaps gain insight into the agonizing decision she was being forced to make.

After the Saturday morning session, the speaker asked for
prayer requests. Without hesitation, though she hadn't
intended to open her heart to anyone, certainly not to the
entire group of women, Maggie stood. She pushed her dark
hair away from her face and with her luminous brown eyes
soft with tears, she told Jodi's story.

"Twenty-one years ago I brought a precious baby girl, my
Jodi, home from the hospital. Just as many of you did, I
dressed her in the softest, pinkest, most ruffly baby dress I
could find. Jodi was beautiful! And I loved her with all my
heart.

"But Jodi was different than other babies. Because of birth
complications, Jodi had been deprived of oxygen for a significant period of time, enough to cause mental retardation.
From the beginning my husband and I knew Jodi would
never have normal intelligence. Oh, I hoped for a miracle—
Jerry and I both did. Maybe if we prayed hard enough, took
her to a different specialist, maybe someone could find a way
to undo what had been done.

"But the miracle never happened. Jodi continued to grow and develop physically, but intellectually she never reached beyond her twelfth year.

"All of this time I carried a load of guilt. If I had taken better care of myself during pregnancy, I thought, maybe my little girl would have been normal; though doctors assured me again and again that this simply wasn't true. But I disagreed. Somehow, some way, I should've known something was wrong. I couldn't get over the feeling that Jodi's condition was my fault.

"As happens with many couples who live through the trauma of having a handicapped child, our marriage began to fall apart. There was simply too much tension for us to deal with. Jerry finally left.

"Caring for Jodi became my life. For twenty-one years I have cared for a child who will never grow up. Until recently she has been in the public school system. And she has been happy being around her fellow students who have similar disabilities—and abilities. But Jodi is now twenty-one and the state no longer has any programs for her.

"And Jodi is lonely. Many of her friends have been moved to homes where they are receiving special training. They learn how to work in fast food chains, or other places, sweeping floors and busing tables. They interact with each other. They aren't lonely."

Maggie paused for a minute, then continued, her voice soft. "I think it's time for me to place Jodi in such a home. But she's my little girl. I'm having a difficult time letting go. I know it's the best thing for her. But I don't know how I will fill the emptiness that will be left without her."

Then, suddenly overcome with emotion, Maggie couldn't speak. And for the briefest moment a reverent silence filled the room. In the back row near the door, a blonde woman stood and walked slowly to where Maggie stood. She hugged Maggie, then asked the audience to pray with her for Maggie and her daughter. As she began to speak, Maggie felt that somehow this woman, whom she had never before met, knew—*really* knew—her heartache and confusion.

Maggie didn't realize it at the time, but she had just met a woman who would become her mentor and possibly the dearest friend she would ever have. After the session broke up, the woman, who cheerfully introduced herself as Beth, invited Maggie to visit with her for a bit in the coffee shop.

Maggie, of course, accepted.

After their cappuccinos were served, Beth began to tell Maggie about her own handicapped child. "I understand what you're going through; I know all about your feelings of guilt and sorrow and depression and discouragement. But I can also tell you that, though the ache never really goes away, there is life for *you* after your nest empties.

"There's a whole world out there for you to explore. You've made the right decision for Jodi. Now you need to make the right decision for you."

Beth went on to tell Maggie about how she had taken the opportunity to discover things about herself that she had forgotten: Who had she been before her child was born? What had been her dearest dreams and desires? She encouraged Maggie to do the same, to reach deep into herself and discover those hidden places that held her own dreams.

This was the beginning of a deep friendship that encompassed spiritual and emotional mentoring and the sharing of ideas that would eventually bring others into their informal support system.

Maggie found a special home for Jodi. Moving her daughter to the facility nearly broke her heart. But Beth's presence, by phone and in person, made it easier to bear, especially during the first lonely days and weeks.

About a month after Jodi's move, Maggie called Beth in excitement. "I want to help other moms who are going through what I went through with Jodi."

"You mean those who are making the same decision you just made?" Beth asked.

"No, I mean before that—from the very beginning. So many couples have no idea what's ahead when they deliver a handicapped baby. They're scared, angry. They feel guilty. They've got so many decisions to make and no experience with the situation they're dealing with." Maggie's voice was earnest. "Maybe I can help."

"That's a wonderful idea, Maggie. Where would you begin?"

"At the hospital. Immediately following the child's birth. I would be there, available to simply listen and offer advice if they asked. But mainly to be a friend who understands."

The two women discussed how they could begin. Beth became as inspired by the idea as Maggie was and decided that she also wanted to help with the counseling. Soon they met, further detailed their plans, and then contacted a local hospital. Their ideas were received enthusiastically.

Not only did Maggie's and Beth's counseling make a difference in the lives of new mothers, the two women also began receiving requests to speak before groups of parents of handicapped children. And after being approached by some of the same parents, they began formal support groups for mothers of handicapped children of all ages.

Recently Maggie told me about her hospital room visits. "With each visit," she said, "I pray, 'Lord, speak through me to this family just as you have spoken to my heart through Jodi's life. Let me share words of comfort, strength, and hope.' Only he knows the words, the thoughts, that will touch each individual family and help them with the pain they feel."

She went on to describe a family she had visited several days earlier. "When I opened the door to the hospital room, I was greeted by the anxious expressions of the new mother and father, expressions of joy and pain mixed together. I could see—no, *feel*—their pain.

"For a few moments I watched the new mother softly stroke her baby's temple with her fingers. Tears coursed down her cheeks, splashing on the tiny blue bundle. I drew closer to the bed and touched the mother's arm. She relaxed and pulled the blanket away from the baby's face.

"A tiny angel slept in her arms. He had a mop of curly blond hair atop a perfectly-shaped head. An immediate response burst from my lips, 'He's beautiful! What's his name?' I asked.

"She said, 'We've decided to call him Justin. Do you really think he's beautiful? You know, he's—' her voice broke off. The smile that had briefly lighted her face disappeared. And her eyes again filled with tears.

"I took her hand and said, 'The words are hard to say at first. I know, because I have a handicapped child too. Don't let the labels get in the way of your love and your hope. There are steps to your adjustment. But there's no timetable. Justin's life is God's precious gift. You will be amazed at how many lives your little angel will touch. I know it's hard to realize now, but Justin will bring deep joy into your life, and into the lives of others.'

"For a moment we watched Justin sleep, then we prayed briefly together. Before I left I gave them my phone number and asked them to call me. I told them I cared, and that I wanted to hear how they were doing. And I told them about the parent support group and invited them to come."

Maggie smiled at me. "They've already called me twice. And they're planning to attend our next support group meeting."

Before our visit was over, I asked Maggie about the inspiration for her dream.

"I realize that your love for Jodi inspired you," I said. "When she first moved out, you were devastated. She had been your whole life. I know many people who would have just let their sorrow and anger consume them. Yet you turned your heartache into something good, something *profoundly* good, for other people."

"You're right," she began, her soft brown eyes filling with tears. "It was my love for my daughter that became my driving force. I wanted to help other parents, particularly moms, who have children with similar handicaps. In every new baby I saw at the hospital I saw my precious Jodi."

She paused, not speaking for a moment. "But I don't think I could have gotten to the point of helping others if it hadn't been for Beth. I really was too consumed by my own negative feelings to be much good to anyone else." She smiled. "God brought Beth into my life at just the right moment. She helped me see beyond myself. She encouraged me to channel my energies outward, instead of letting them eat me up on the inside. And I knew that she understood better than anyone what I was going through; she'd been there. She'd lived it. And she'd made it through."

"She was your hero?"

"Oh, yes," Maggie said without hesitation. "She really was, and is, as the song says, 'the wind beneath my wings.'"

## Other Heroes

Our heroes, or role models, don't have to be people we know. They can be historical or contemporary figures, male or female, dead or alive. They simply need to be people who have had dreams as big as ours—or bigger—and who have lived their dreams.

Mark Twain once said, "Biographies are but the clothes and buttons of the man—the biography of the man himself cannot be written." Still, we can examine the "clothes and buttons" of our chosen heroes, find out how they came to "wear" their dreams, and learn from them as we "wear" our own dreams.

Helen Keller is a source of inspiration to dreamer and nondreamer alike. She once said about her own dreams, "One can never consent to creep when one feels an impulse to soar." And if we should take the time to study her life, we will also soar on wings like eagles, crying with her in the anguish of her frustrations, rejoicing with her in her triumphs.

Helen Keller was born in 1880, blind, deaf, and mute, yet she learned to read, write, and speak, eventually graduating *cum laude* from Radcliffe College. Her life has come to represent the most extraordinary accomplishment ever made in the education of persons so severely handicapped. Her work with her teacher, mentor, and friend, Anne Mansfield Sullivan, is also a story of moving and profound inspiration.

Another inspiring historical figure is Harriet Tubman, born into slavery in 1820. In 1849, Harriet escaped from a plantation on the eastern shore of Maryland. On her way north she was helped by people who were part of the Underground Railroad. The following year, she returned to Maryland to guide members of her family north to freedom. She soon became one of the "railroad's" most active "conductors." She made frequent trips into the Deep South to bring out runaway slaves. Her journeys usually began on Saturday night, giving the fugitives more than a day before their owners discovered their departure and sounded the alarm for their return.

After the Fugitive Slave Law in 1850, she guided escaping slaves into Canada. Despite huge rewards for her capture, Harriet Tubman helped more than three hundred slaves escape. She was tough and single-minded in the pursuit of her dream. She maintained military discipline among her followers, knowing their lives hung in the balance. She often forced the weary or the fainthearted ahead by threatening them with a loaded revolver.

Yet in spite of her tough exterior, she understood very well the loneliness and apprehension many runaways felt after they arrived in the North. She identified with those she helped, saying, "I was free, but there was no one to welcome me to the land of freedom. I was a stranger in a strange land. . . ."

During the Civil War, Harriet served the Union forces as a nurse and spy. She became friends with some of the best-known figures of her time, including Ralph Waldo Emerson. John Brown referred to her in his letters as "one of the best and bravest persons on this continent—*General* Tubman we call her."

Harriet Tubman died March 10, 1913, leaving a legacy of courage and faith in her God.

How about contemporary heroes, women who have pursued dreams for their own fulfillment as well as women who have fulfilled their dreams to help others? There are those who are little known and those who are well known. Yet if we examine their lives, we see that they share with us the courage to overcome adversity and the dedication to pursue their dreams.

Charlayne Hunter-Gault is a woman who has pursued such a dream. She first dreamed of becoming a journalist when she was twelve years old living in Atlanta, Georgia. Her unlikely "hero" was the blue-eyed, red-haired comic-strip character Brenda Starr. Unlikely, because she was a fictional character. Even more unlikely because, as an African American living in the still segregated South, Charlayne faced the difficulties of a prejudiced world.

But Charlayne was not to be discouraged and, at sixteen, ignoring the advice of her high school counselor, she applied to the University of Georgia's School of Journalism. In the school's 175-year history, a black applicant had never been admitted.

It took two years for Charlayne to finally realize the first short-term goal of her big dream. In 1961, she was finally admitted, one of the two first black students in the university's history. She walked to her classes alone, through the jeers and taunts—even tear gas from the riots outside her dorm—protesting her presence.

Since 1978, Charlayne has held the position of correspondent and substitute anchor on the *MacNeil/Lehrer News*

*Hour* on PBS, one of the most respected news programs in the nation, then as well as today.

She has received an array of impressive awards, including two National News and Documentary Emmy Awards, the Newswomen's Club of New York Front Page Award, the American Women in Radio and Television Award, the Women of Achievement Award, two Public Broadcasting System Awards, and the Peabody Award in 1986 for her five-part series from South Africa on apartheid.

When we watch Charlayne in action, as I recently did when she interviewed Wangari Matthai, the Kenyan environmental activist, we celebrate Charlayne's intelligent, articulate, and refreshing perspective. Wangari Matthai (another hero!) has inspired thousands of women in Africa to plant ten million trees. They receive fifty cents for every tree that survives three months. The subsistence also gives the women a feeling of empowerment as well as a way to change their world for the better. Wangari Matthai sees the women as nurturers with a natural instinct to nurture the earth.

Charlayne Hunter-Gault, with her intense love of life, is a very concrete and worthy hero for us all. As unlikely a hero as a comic-strip character might be, it allowed the young Charlayne to dream dreams and to live her dreams. Charlayne says the following about Brenda Starr, her hero: "I never could have become a journalist if I hadn't had the capacity to fantasize, because in those days there weren't any black women—or men, for that matter—working in mainstream media, so-called 'role models.'

"My role model, I guess, developed out of a fantasy life I had with my dolls and the comic strips. Brenda Starr was my fantasy role model. I loved this life of hers and thought it was very exciting. If I had not been given to fantasy, I never could have imagined myself doing something like that because there were roles set up for us, women like me, we knew 'our place.' Fantasizing enabled me to see beyond the limits of Jim Crow, and while I didn't know how I was going to get there, I felt that I *could* get there and I fantasized about getting there and the way was made."

Throughout the country, women viewers write to Charlayne Hunter-Gault to thank her for bringing a woman's perspective to the daily news, to coverage of the Gulf War, the Los Angeles riots, the recent South Africa elections, to race relations and women's issues. And we add our voice to theirs: Thank you, Charlayne, for having the courage to dream! We're all the richer for it.

Another life of inspiration is that of novelist Isabel Allende. Isabel was born in Lima, Peru, where her father, a Chilean diplomat, was posted. During her early years, she lived in Chile, Bolivia, Europe, and the Middle East. At fifteen she returned to Chile, completed her education, and became a journalist.

In September of 1973, Isabel's life was irrevocably changed when a violent military coup resulted in the death of her uncle, then-President Salvador Allende. She says of that time, "I remember that day as one of the worst days in my life. Everything changed in twenty-four hours.

"I stayed in Chile thinking that democracy would return. As I became more and more involved in helping people and hiding them, there came a point when I had to leave. I felt so threatened; I was so scared."

Frightened and desperate, Isabel escaped and went into exile with her two children. She eventually ended up in California, where she lives today with her husband and her daughter, Paula.

Isabel's first book was published when she was thirty-nine, and since then she has had two more published. All have received worldwide critical acclaim.

Isabel's life has been full of adventure, challenge, and success, but she also carried a nearly unbearable heartache. Her daughter, Paula, has been in a coma for the past few years, the result of complications from the treatment of a genetic disease called porphyria. When Paula, only twenty-eight and a newlywed, fell ill, Isabel flew to Spain to be with her. When Isabel found out that the prognosis for recovery was not hopeful, she made the decision to bring her daughter to her home in California where family members could give her round-the-clock care.

She speaks of the pain of her experience with Paula as being deeper than any she's ever known. "I have been in pain and been in difficult situations before, but I have never been in a situation in which I was *totally* out of control. I don't have control over anything. I can't even run away from it. When I was desperate in Chile during the military coup, and I was terribly afraid, I ran away with my kids. I took everybody into exile. But now I have to go through all the pain, through hell and back. . . .

"What I can bring back is my memory of Paula—my own perspective as a mother—because I cannot reach her."

Isabel says that passion and love are her reasons for living. They are perhaps what comforted her in the past and continue to support her survival in the present. The original meaning of the word *passion,* it is said, is the ability to endure suffering.

For those of us who aspire to write, our hero, Isabel Allende, says this to us: "When I begin a book, I usually feel there is something growing in the womb, not in the mind. . . . Usually, I don't know where that first sentence leads, or what will come next, but it's like opening a door and you enter into an unknown place and things begin to unfold as you give them time.

"I tell people, 'If you want to write, write! Don't study. Don't try to copy anybody else, just write. And by doing it, you'll get there if you have a vocation.' People think that writing is sitting down and writing a book that will be famous immediately. Most of the time writing is just hard work with no recompense. So if you are able to get through that long period during which you are starving and you aren't published or even receiving any feedback, then you really have a vocation; you really want to write, so do it."

There is another woman in the world today who, above most—if not all—others, inspires us to the unselfish giving of ourselves.

The woman? Mother Teresa of Calcutta.

Mother Teresa has said, "I know God will not give me anything I can't handle. I just wish that he didn't trust me so much."

His trust in her is evident to the world. Her life is an inspiration to us all.

Mother Teresa was born Agnes Gonxha Bojaxhiu in 1910 in Albania. Her father was a grocer, and she grew up in a modest home. At age eighteen, Agnes made the decision to study to be a teacher at the Institute of the Blessed Virgin Mary in Ireland. She trained there for only six weeks before sailing for India.

Mother Teresa's heart was profoundly moved by the poverty and medical needs of the people in India. After teaching for a few years, she requested nurse's training and permission to work with the poor of Calcutta. The permission was granted, and after studying nursing, Mother Teresa moved into the slums.

City authorities, at her request, gave her the pilgrim hostel near Kali's temple. Other women, inspired by her dedication and touched by the need, flocked to her aid. Medical dispensaries and outdoor schools were organized. In 1948 she founded the Order of the Missionaries of Charity—a Roman Catholic congregation of women dedicated to the poor, especially the destitute of Calcutta.

Mother Teresa became an Indian citizen and, with her Indian nuns, designed and adopted the sari as their habit.

Under Mother Teresa's guidance, the order opened medical centers to help the blind, the aged, lepers, the physically handicapped, and the dying. She led the Missionaries of Charity in the building of a leper colony called Shanti Nagar (Town of Peace).

In 1963, the Indian government awarded Mother Teresa the "Lord of the Lotus" for her services to the people of India. In 1964, on his trip to India, Pope Paul VI presented her with his ceremonial limousine, which, true to her humble spirit, she immediately raffled to help finance her leper colony.

In the 1970s, the Missionaries of Charity numbered nearly seven hundred nuns who operated sixty centers in Calcutta and more than seventy worldwide, including foundations in Ceylon, Tanzania, Jordan, Venezuela, Great Britain, and Australia.

By 1970, her foundation in Calcutta alone had saved nearly eight thousand destitute outcasts from death. And today, through her worldwide foundations, it is estimated that tens of thousands of lives have been saved—all because one woman dared to dream and dared to explore becoming *all* that God would have her become.

Mother Teresa has given her life to help others—at great risk to herself, physically and emotionally. Yet with dedication to her dream, her calling, she continues on, tirelessly, unceasingly, reaching out to help alleviate the pain and suffering in the world around her.

## A Hero to Live in Your Heart

Whether your hero is someone you know personally, someone you have become acquainted with as you begin to live your dream, or someone you have become aware of through biographical readings, this person belongs in your heart.

Ask yourself how your hero can inspire you to take steps in the direction of living your dreams.

In your journal, write your hero's name and list those attributes you admire in her (or him!).

Take time to examine these strengths. If you know the person well, you might already know (or be willing to ask) how those strengths came into existence. If you are reading a biography of a historical figure, analyze personality traits and also look for strengths.

Look for the life-challenges your hero had to overcome. Are they anything like your own life-challenges? If so, how?

What barriers existed in your hero's life? Specifically, how did she turn them into positive energies working for her as she pursued her dream?

Write a purpose statement from what you know about your hero to give yourself a better idea of the processes she went through in finding and living her dream.

If your hero (specifically a historical figure) were sitting and visiting with you, what do you think she would tell you about your own dream? What do you think she would say about overcoming your own barriers?

What are your hero's flaws? (If you are reading a good biography, they will be evident right alongside the positive qualities.) Examine the personality flaws you see in your living mentor-hero.

Rejoice that she has them!

*Rejoice?*

Yes, rejoice! For when we realize that our heroes became heroes, *flaws and all*, it gives us hope. They're human just as we are. We don't have to be perfect to fulfill our dreams.

It takes courage and passion to pursue your dream. It takes commitment to live your dream. If you look carefully, you'll see that heroes, right alongside their flaws, have these qualities.

And so do you!

~~~

## Reflections

You, however, know all about my teaching, my way of life,
my purpose, faith, patience, love, endurance.

2 TIMOTHY 3:10

This week, ask God to bring into your life those who will
help you dream. Thank him for their positive influence in
your life and in the lives of others. Rejoice in their attributes,
especially their courage. Be glad for their dream pursuits; be
glad for their flaws! Celebrate who they are to you.

*Dear Jesus, thank you for those people who help us dream
by sharing with us their wisdom, insights, struggles, and
triumphs. We are challenged by their example; we are
blessed by their friendship.*

# 9

# Committing to Our Dreams

*Put all your eggs in one basket and WATCH THAT BASKET.*

MARK TWAIN

*S*peaking of dream commitment, Sheila Graham said, "You can have anything you want if you want it desperately enough. You must want it with an inner exuberance that erupts through the skin and joins the energy that created the world." Add to that Henry Ford's words, "You can't build a reputation on what you're *going* to do."

W. H. Murray (of the Scottish Himalayan Expedition) wrote:

> Until one is committed, there is hesitancy, the chance to draw back, always ineffectiveness. Concerning all acts of

169

initiative (and creation) there is one elementary truth, the
ignorance of which kills countless ideas and splendid plans:
that the moment one definitely commits oneself, then
Providence moves too. All sorts of things occur to help
one that would never otherwise have occurred. A whole
stream of events issues from the decision, raising in one's
favor all manner of unforeseen incidents and meetings and
material assistance, which no man could have dreamed
would have come his way. I have learned a deep respect
for one of Goethe's couplets: *Whatever you can do, or
dream you can, begin it. Boldness has genius, power and
magic in it.*[1]

## Commitment: A Promise We Make to Ourselves

Commitment is our pledge to ourselves to act on our word.
And the test of our commitment is action. Until we begin to
move toward our dream—to act—we are not truly committed to our dream.

Our dream is precious and serious. God has been in the
process of our dream discovery from its inception. Our commitment, to him and to ourselves, cannot be casual. And it
is not a one-time occurrence. We must choose to act daily
on the personal goals leading to our dream's fulfillment.

We have carefully written out our purpose and our dreams.
Living our dream is a commitment we plan to keep. We will
live with its results for the rest of our lives.

Our lives will change for the better—if we keep our commitment to ourselves.

Or our lives will forever remain the same—if we don't keep
our commitment to ourselves.

## Time + Action = Commitment

We've made a commitment. We're ready and raring to go.
But . . . what do we do next? How do we begin?

The equation Time + Action = Commitment first leads us to consider time and how we can use it or be used by it. (Be patient: Time will lead us into action.)

### The Value of Time

We can make time work *for* us, or we can let it become "a file that wears (us down) and makes no noise" (H. C. Bohn).

Time can rob us of our big dream.

Or time can enrich us, goading us into action as we commit to our big dream.

It's up to us to decide which it will be.

Let's think about how time can work for us in committing to our dream.

#### Developing a Timeline and Setting Measurable Goals

Say your dream is to return to school and complete your degree. You've figured out the number of units you earned twenty-five years ago. You've wisely sought the help of a college counselor who told you that you still have more than ninety units to complete for your bachelor's degree.

Quick arithmetic tells you that if you attend school full-time for three years (provided you have met all prerequisites and can get into the needed classes), you will graduate with your B.A.

*Three years,* you groan. *That's a long time. I'll be forty-seven years old!*

I've got good news.

The three years are going to pass anyway. And you're going to be forty-seven—whether or not you pursue your dream.

You may as well be forty-seven years old with a bachelor's degree (or any dream fulfilled) as be forty-seven without it.

Knowledge of time's irretrievable passage can goad you into action if you use it to set measurable goals, understanding that you are working toward the final goal—fulfillment of your big dream.

Let's consider how this works.

When World Vision, the international relief and development agency, begins a field project—whether in the United States or internationally—the staff first begins by setting obtainable and measurable goals. (Later, we'll take a look at how this can serve as a model for individuals.)

As an example, during the mid-1980s a devastating drought and famine struck Ethiopia. Hundreds of thousands of children and families died. World Vision began a monumental relief effort. They saved thousands of lives by providing emergency food, water, and medical care.

When the immediate emergency subsided, many relief agencies left the area. But World Vision remained, because they had a dream: World Vision staff wanted to work with the Ethiopian people to ensure that a drought and famine of this magnitude would never again decimate lives and lands. They wanted to reverse the process: turn the once lush and verdant land, now a giant dust bowl, back to its original state. They even had the audacity to dream it could be better! It would be drought-proof.

*Drought-proof?*

What a dream!

World Vision chose the dusty, desolate, and colorless Ansokia Valley to consider for the project. They brought in water experts to discuss well digging and irrigation, agriculture experts to discuss drought-resistant crops, community development experts to discuss solutions to economic needs, health care experts to discuss medical health and nutrition needs, and education experts to discuss providing schools for the village children.

From the beginning, community leaders joined with World Vision staff members in the decision-making process. Guess what they did? They set measurable goals for the Ansokia Valley Project.

It would be a five-year project. The objective at the end of five years was to have developed the region agriculturally and economically to the point of stability and sustainability. And run by the community members themselves.

The long-range goals included:

- 100 wells would be dug (with an estimated 90 percent wet well success rate).
- 1,000 villagers would receive training in how to operate and repair the wells.
- 10,000 tree seedlings would be planted for reforestation to guard against the dust bowl effect.
- 25,000 families would plant kitchen gardens, learning better farming and irrigation techniques and using drought-resistant seeds and plants.
- 100,000 children would receive immunizations against childhood diseases.
- 50,000 parents would receive training on how to provide better health care and nutrition for their families.

Notice how concrete and measurable these goals are.

These long-range goals were divided into yearly increments, then divided again into quarterly goals. Each quarter after the project's beginning, the managers measured exactly how many of the goals had been met—and how many had not been met. Sometimes goals had to be adjusted because of unforeseen circumstances. (For example, heavy rains delayed the digging of wells during one quarter.)

At the end of the five-year project an amazing transformation had taken place in the Ansokia Valley: Where once the pall of death had hung in the dusty air and the only sounds had been those of the mourning as they buried their dead, now the green valley was alive with the sounds of birds singing and people cheerfully tending their farms and the sounds of happy children's voices as they walked to school.

What made the dramatic difference in the Ansokia Valley? It wasn't just the dreams of change—the dream was the foundation of change. It was the decisive action of forward-looking people who moved in increments of short-term goals to bring about long-term change.

Think, too, about the long-term nature of the impossible dream: The five years following the great Ethiopian drought would have passed anyway, with or without World Vision's intervention.

Was it worth spending five years pursuing a dream to make the lives of thousands of people better? Of course, the answer is a resounding *yes*.

But consider this: Is it worth spending whatever time it may take you to pursue your personal dream?

The answer here must also be a resounding *yes!*

You have probably guessed your next action in your dream pursuit. You're right: It's time to develop your own timeline and measurable goals.

Please open your journal. At the top of a blank page, write your purpose statement. Underneath that, write your dream. (Remember to use the more positive "I am" rather than "I want.")

Draw a line horizontally across the page. (This is your timeline.) On the left-hand side write today's date. On the right-hand side write the date you project that your dream will be fulfilled. Your line should look something like this:

(date)                                                           (date)
├──────────────────────────────────────────────────────────┤

Next, draw increments along the timeline on which to place your short-term goals. Number these increments. Then below the timeline, define your short-term goals according to their number.

Say your dream is to learn to fly. Your timeline would look something like this:

(date) (date)

1.          2. 3.               4.     5.     6.

1. Enroll in ground school.
2. Complete ground school.
3. Begin flying lessons.
4. Complete first cross-country solo.
5. Pass FAA exam.
6. Dream fulfilled: I have pilot's license!!!

Keep in mind as you determine short-term goals that they need to be specific, measurable, and obtainable. Specific and measurable, so that you can monitor your achievements as you "live" your timeline. Obtainable, so that vaguely worded or overly ambitious goals won't discourage you.

This is your big dream. Take plenty of time to prayerfully consider your course: You are mapping out the journey of a lifetime.

Then take a deep breath.

And prepare to act on your dream.

### The Value of Action

"There are risks and costs to a program of action," John F. Kennedy once said, "but they are far less than the long-range risks and costs of comfortable inaction."

You may not realize it, but you have already begun to act on your dream. You have been moving toward your dream with each page you turned in this book, with each journal entry you have completed. With each minute that passes, you are moving toward fulfillment of your dream.

But the momentum must continue. For it to do so, three emotional mind-sets must be activated:

1. You must ruthlessly guard your time.
2. You must do the work of your dream.

3. You must not be afraid of your mistakes.

Let's look at number one: *You must ruthlessly guard your time.* To successfully dream our big dream, we must now let go of the things in our lives that consume our time and energy.

Take a few moments to quietly consider the distractions in your life. Some may be positive distractions. Others, negative.

My friend Cathy, artistic and creative, dreamed of opening a country crafts shop (she even had a name: Country Crazy) in her small town in the Midwest. For years she had designed and sewn intricately patterned quilts, needlepoint stitcheries, and counted cross-stitch wall hangings. She won blue ribbons for her work in the county fair. In fact, throughout the northern part of the state, her work is known and admired—even in demand.

Cathy had taught third grade in a local elementary school for twenty-three years. She enjoyed working with eight-year-olds and had passed on to many of her students her love for handicrafts, design, and creativity.

Cathy didn't want to give up teaching; not only was it fulfilling, but it would someday provide a good retirement income. She wanted to do both: continue teaching *and* pursue her dream to open a crafts shop of her own. But was it possible? Let's take a look at her dilemma.

To fulfill her big dream, Cathy had mapped out these short-term goals for herself:

1. Take beginning and advanced classes in small-business management at local community college.
2. Create three hundred pieces of original designs for display and supply in the Country Crazy shop.
3. Contact and give artistic guidance to other artisans who might be interested in consignment sales through Country Crazy.

4. Find a trusted worker to "mind the shop" when she could not physically be there.
5. Find a shop to lease.
6. Save for six-month coverage of lease.

This was a "tall order" for dream fulfillment. But with determination, it could be done. Except that . . . Cathy had distractions that threatened to keep her from living her dream.

Cathy volunteered for wonderful and worthy causes. On Saturdays, she helped cook at a local senior citizen's center. On Sundays, she taught Sunday school in the morning and played golf with her husband in the afternoon. She also had let the folks at the senior center know that she was available weekdays after school to drive those without cars to appointments or to the grocery store. (They regularly took her up on her offer.)

Obviously, Cathy couldn't do it all. To live her big dream, she needed to let go (even temporarily) of those things that distracted her, that kept her from acting on her dream.

None of us can do it all. We have to make choices on the journey toward our dream. Sometimes *difficult* choices.

We will be tested by our distractions. Be prepared: Some of them *seem* so worthy, just as Cathy's were. Still others will be intertwined with comfort zones, ours as well as those of people close to us.

It will be up to us to decide the worthiness of our sacred dream.

Next, *You must do the work of your dream.* Thomas Edison said, "Opportunity is missed by most people because it is dressed in overalls and looks like work." The very word *dream* conjures up a velvety, ethereal image: a soft and comfortable magic-carpet flight during which we are set down in Paradise; an effortless fantasy in which we are transported from dreaming to dream in one fell swoop.

Yet the action required in pursuing our dream couldn't be farther from that image. In reality, pursuing dreams is hard work. And the work never ends. As we achieve one short-term goal, we will begin working toward another. And another. And another.

But don't be disheartened. William James observed, "If an unusual necessity forces us onward, a surprising thing occurs. The fatigue gets worse up to a certain point, when, gradually or suddenly, it passes away and we are fresher than before!"

People who run or bike long distances often report that they reach a point where they feel they can't go on, only to push through it and continue with a new level of energy. "We have evidently tapped a new level of energy," William James continues. "There may be layer after layer of this experience, a third and fourth 'wind.' We find amounts of ease and power that we never dreamed ourselves to own, sources of strength habitually not taxed, because habitually we never push through the obstruction of fatigue."

Back to my friend Cathy. Once she committed to her big dream, she ruthlessly cleared her path of distractions.

The process took emotional energy. She hadn't realized how many people counted on her volunteer services (though she had suspected for some time that in some cases she was being taken for granted).

The meaning of treading on someone else's comfort zone became vividly clear as she committed to her dream. Her husband, though supportive of her dream to open Country Crazy, initially felt hurt that they could no longer play golf every Sunday afternoon. It took time for him to get comfortable with his new "comfort zone," to understand her time restraints and dedication to her dream. He soon began to get caught up in the excitement of the dream and even offered to contact a realtor and do the preliminary legwork in hunting for a good location for the shop.

Then Cathy moved on to the hard work involved in preparing for the opening of Country Crazy. She developed an eighteen-month timeline. It would take her two semesters to complete the business management classes. During the same time, she needed to complete three hundred quilt, needlepoint, and cross-stitch pieces. She further broke it down to sixteen per month, or four per week.

She contacted a number of other artisans and arranged to meet with them once a month to give them direction on the pieces they were creating for her shop. She added to her schedule homework for business management education.

Cathy was used to hard work. Teaching third graders takes an abundance of energy. But focusing energy on her big dream brought an even greater loss of physical stamina. Just one month into her first semester, and sixteen pieces into her dream, Cathy felt so tired that she wondered if her dream was worth it.

"I don't know if I've got what it takes for the long haul," she told me. "I've always been active, but this is different. Plus I spend at least three hours a day working on the pieces for the shop."

"You haven't gotten your second wind?" I asked tentatively.

She laughed. "*Second?* I'll need three or four to get me through this!"

"It'll come. Believe me," I said, hoping it would be soon. "Just wait."

A few weeks later, Cathy called me. She sounded excited.

"I've met this great group of folks at school. Several of them are in the process of starting their own business."

"You're not tired anymore?" I couldn't resist asking, though I could tell by the exuberance in her voice that something had changed.

She didn't speak for a moment. I wondered if she had forgotten about the exhaustion she'd earlier told me about.

Then she said, "You know, when I felt the most tired, I'd lost sight of my dream. I was focusing on the work; and believe me, there's still an overabundance of that." She laughed. "But when I began telling the other students in my business class about my dream, I got excited all over again. I could see they were excited for me."

*Aha!* I thought. *Mentoring at work.*

Cathy went on. "I still get tired, but when I think about the purpose of my work—that it's to make my dream a reality—suddenly I *do* get a second wind." She chuckled. "And a third. And a fourth."

There's no doubt about it, any dream worth dreaming will draw energy from us—physical, intellectual, and emotional. So we need to be prepared—body, soul, and spirit.

At this stage in your big dream pursuit, don't forget to nurture yourself so that greater energy will be yours. It might be a good idea to review chapter three on caring for yourself. This is a time of your life when nutrition and physical and mental exercise will pay off.

After all, you're in training: You need to be in tip-top shape for the work that lies ahead.

And you need to focus on your dream.

This brings us to number three: *You must not be afraid of your mistakes.* Aristotle said, "For the things we have to learn before we can do them, we learn by doing them." If we learn by doing, doesn't that leave us wide open to making mistakes? That's a frightening thought!

We've dared to dream.

We've prepared to dream.

Now we're ready to actually do it. Take the plunge. Actually *act.*

Then we step out and make a mistake. We blow it. Bigtime.

Where does that leave us?

Take heart. I have good news about mistake making. Theodore Roosevelt said it well: "Far better it is to dare mighty things, to win glorious triumphs even though checkered by failure, than to rank with those poor spirits who neither enjoy nor suffer much because they live in the gray twilight that knows neither victory nor defeat."

And Winston Churchill said, in speaking of a mistake's aftermath, "Men stumble over the truth from time to time, but most pick themselves up and hurry off as if nothing happened."

Whenever we stumble over the truth and hurry off, it's a mistake. But it's not the stumble that is the mistake. (The stumble can bring truth, learning, to our consciousness.) It's the *hurrying off* without learning the stumble's lesson that is the mistake.

We can and do make mistakes. That's a given. Most of us know the feeling well: sweaty palms. Heaviness in our chests. The instant replay in our minds telling us that, instead of what we said or did, we *should* have said this or *should* have done that.

But mistakes are opportunities to learn, to grow, to gain knowledge that will help us find success next time. Freud said, "From error to error, one discovers the entire truth."

Mistakes are stepping stones, "from error to error," on the way to our dream. If we're not willing to take necessary steps toward our dream, with the understanding that some of them will be mistakes, we'll stay within the confines of our comfort zone. After all, it *is* more comfortable to play it safe. But we'll wonder why we never seem to move closer to our dream.

Several months ago I saw my friend Cathy again. I, of course, asked immediately how her dream pursuit was going.

A flash of worry crossed her face, then quickly disappeared as she smiled. "Well, actually . . ."

I waited for her to continue.

"Right after I saw you last, Sue, my sister-in-law, asked if she could go into business with me. She was so excited about my plans. She's a great seamstress and her offer to help seemed attractive at the time. But now, I'm having second thoughts."

Ah. Now I knew whence came the worried expression I'd seen earlier. "What seems to be wrong?"

Cathy went on. "It's fun having someone share the work, but she has a way of taking over . . ." Her voice dropped off.

"How do you mean?"

"Sue's a very strong personality. She's trying to run things her own way, even at this stage. I can only imagine what it will be like when we open the shop." Cathy shook her head slowly, then sighed. "I don't know what to do."

"Can you tell Sue that you've made a mistake, that you'd prefer doing this on your own?" I asked.

"I'm afraid that it will cause family problems. It makes it worse that we're related."

Cathy and I discussed her options:

1. She could give up her dream, thus dissolving the headaches of her "partnership" with her sister-in-law.
2. She could continue letting Sue share—*take over*—her dream, probably destroying Cathy's joy and enthusiasm in the process.
3. She could continue working toward her dream *alone*, letting Sue know that this is a personal dream that Cathy alone must fulfill. (This could be a delicate and potentially hurtful process. However, she could try encouraging her sister-in-law to explore her own personal dream discovery. Cathy could also suggest being available as Sue's friend and mentor.)
4. She could learn from her mistake.

Cathy chose the third course of action. Initially, her sister-in-law was hurt at her exclusion from Cathy's plans to open Country Crazy. Cathy had never told Sue that the shop was her big dream, something that was very personal and could only be fulfilling if she made it happen *alone*. But after Cathy explained how sacred and special this dream was to her, Sue understood. She also took Cathy's advice and began exploring her own dreams.

Cathy also chose number four: She chose to learn from her mistake, to use it as an "error to error" stepping stone toward her dream. As soon as Cathy took action (handled the problem with her sister-in-law), she got right back to work on her dream with new determination to see Country Crazy become a successful reality.

She also found that by successfully working through her first major mistake, she didn't fear the next mistake as much. And Cathy discovered the process held an added bonus: her comfort zone had expanded as she discovered and dealt with her error.

Mistakes point out to us what we need to learn. Welcome them as aids to your dream education. Analyze them and ask yourself, "How could I have done better?" or, "How could I have avoided this error?" or, "How can I learn from this opportunity?" Then pat yourself on the back for your ability to recognize the lesson in your mistake.

Fred Astaire once said, "The higher up you go, the more mistakes you're allowed. Right at the top, if you make enough of them, it's considered to be your style."

You're committing to your dream—taking actions that by necessity will bring about mistakes.

Take Mr. Astaire's words to heart: Celebrate your "style."

And be sure to smile cagily to yourself as you do so, because only you will know the difference!

## Time + Action = Success

We began this section with the equation: Time + Action = Commitment.

Let's add to that Time + Action = Success.

Following the equation, we have developed a timeline and set short-term goals. We have moved into action, facing whatever is ahead: challenges and mistakes as well.

We have made a commitment.

And success will follow.

It's vitally important at this stage of our dream commitment to remember the Source of our success: our living God and Savior, through whom our strength and commitment flow.

Besides managing our time, getting rid of distractions, gearing up for hard work, and moving through the frustrations of making mistakes, we need to return daily to that place of solitude where we can renew our strength and refresh our enthusiasm.

Daily, trust Christ with your hopes and your dreams.

Trust him with your concerns. Ask him for guidance and wisdom when you face challenges . . . when you make mistakes.

Be still before him. Listen for him to speak to you in the silence of your heart.

Ask him to be with you on *today's* journey toward your dream.

Celebrate the wonder of where you are on your journey.

Rejoice with him in your discoveries.

Commit your time to him. Ask him to help you distinguish those things that are important to living your dream— and that will glorify him in the process.

Ask him to help you weed out the distractions from your day.

Then open your journal (and open it again each morning for thirty days, then for another thirty, and thirty more, and so on . . . until your dream is fulfilled) and write down those specific actions that you will take today toward fulfilling your dream.

Ask God to be with you as you take these actions.

Move into your day with the stillness and strength that your time alone with him will bring.

Celebrate the equation that your commitment and his power is creating in your life: My Time + My Action = My Success.

Whatever you can do, or dream you can, begin it. Boldness has genius, power and magic in it.

GOETHE
*FAUST*

❧❧❧

## Reflections

Know therefore that the LORD your God is God; he is the faithful God, keeping his covenant of love to a thousand generations of those who love him and keep his commands.

DEUTERONOMY 7:9

This week, dwell on the meaning of commitment in your life and in the lives of those you admire. Remember especially the example of God's commitment to us: It is eternal. It is a covenant of love and faithfulness. Celebrate his everlasting compassion toward you. This God is with you as you dream! Praise him for his faithfulness!

*Dear Lord, the depths of your love and faithfulness are more than we can begin to comprehend. May we be mindful of your presence as we act on our dreams. Give us strength in our struggles. Give us humbleness of heart in our triumphs. Give us joy through our dreams.*

# 10

# It's Time to Live Our Dreams!

*Those who are wise will instruct many.*

DANIEL 11:33

*From everyone who has been given much, much will be demanded; and from the one who has been entrusted with much, much more will be asked.*

LUKE 12:48

The best dreams are those that live and breathe and continue to grow as we grow. A dream that never dies stays alive in two ways:

1. When we achieve our dream, we may find another related dream just beyond the horizon.
2. A dream that is given away never dies.

## Related Dreams

*When we achieve our dream, we may find another related dream just beyond the horizon.* We didn't see it until we fulfilled the original dream. We may continue the process of setting new goals and dreaming new dreams until we're ninety-three!

I've got a secret for you. (But maybe you've already guessed it.) *The process of pursuing the dream brings greater fulfillment than the achievement of the dream.* Robert Townsend said it this way, "Getting there isn't half the fun—it's all the fun."

Besides the joy we find while pursuing our goals and achieving our dreams, we also find an unexpected treasure: We learn volumes about ourselves—who we are inside; the discovery of long-forgotten hopes and dreams; the unearthing of long-buried traits that helped us along the way, such as discipline, focus, enthusiasm, creativity, passion, delight, curiosity.

And we continue to discover these inner riches as we pursue new dreams.

Do you remember the story I related in chapter seven about my childhood friend Marihelen? She dreamed of graduating from college even though she knew she had to overcome great difficulties (a learning disability). She achieved that dream.

Then she pursued the next dream that appeared on the horizon. She enrolled again at the university to go for her master's degree in educational counseling. She achieved that dream.

Then she pursued the next dream that appeared on the horizon.

Marihelen, now forty-seven years old, had a B.A. in liberal arts and an M.A. in counseling. It was the 1990s—not a good time to be looking for work in California (her home state), not a good time to be looking for work in the field of education, and *really* not a good time to be looking for work if you're forty-seven and have no experience in the field.

But Marihelen, rising to the new challenge, dared to dream again. And as she did, she discovered a new treasure trove of qualities within herself: tenacity, spunk, discipline, joy, passion, perseverance.

Her inner riches were primed and ready for living her new dream. But more about this dream later.

Her experience illustrates Samuel Johnson's observation, "Life affords no higher pleasure than that of surmounting difficulties, passing from one step of success to another, forming new wishes and seeing them gratified."

As we pursue new dreams, we experience the excitement of beginning the process afresh. We further expand our comfort zones—sometimes pushing them to new limits, dreaming broader and deeper dreams than we ever thought were possible.

We test the same old barriers—fear, guilt, unworthiness, discouragement, procrastination—and we find, though they are still formidable, we *can* fly over them. We set new goals, a new timeline, and we lose ourselves, joyously, enthusiastically, though perhaps with trembling, in living our new dream.

We test our strength to again persevere, and we thrill to that inner Voice that tells us he is with us, empowering us, molding us, using us as we dream. We discover new wonders within our limitless storehouse of definable (and sometimes undefinable) qualities, tenacity and joy among them.

And from this storehouse that now includes the richness of *experience* we find ourselves unable to contain a fresh and contagious joy. We want others to dream dreams and pursue their dreams. We want to help them, teach them, mentor them as they dream . . . which leads us to the second way we keep our dreams alive.

*A dream that is given away never dies.* We give from an inner storehouse of resources. Whatever we have collected in the process of attaining our dream is that which we have to give away.

Let's review for a moment what we have collected as we dared to dream.

Open your journal and review, page by page, those sacred thoughts and prayers about yourself and your desires.

Begin with your view of *solitude*. You have learned to celebrate your new solitude rather than view it as loneliness, abandonment, an obstacle, or an enemy. Instead, solitude is a gift to be cherished, to be used. Lift your heart in celebration of this gift today.

Next, take a look at those things you've written about your *creation*. Review your meditations on self-love and about nurturing yourself physically, intellectually, emotionally, and spiritually.

Reveal your thoughts on expanding your *comfort zone*. How did you feel as you worked through your discomfort when faced with the barriers: fear, guilt, unworthiness, discouragement, and procrastination? How do you feel now that you have learned to use them as energy for change? Be glad! Rejoice in your discoveries!

Take a long time looking over your *gifts*. Meditate for a few moments as you read your *purpose* sentence. Read carefully those sentences you've written about who you are. Lift them up in prayer and rejoice that God has created you *just the way you are!*

Review your list of wants. Rejoice in the *dream* you chose. Celebrate the way you are actively moving toward—living— your dream at this moment.

Celebrate your *hero*. Think about who she is, how she discovered her dream and pursued it with courage, flaws and all. If she is a living mentor, helping you today as you dream, make a mental note to call her and thank her for the inspiration she has been to you. If your hero is a historical or contemporary figure you don't know personally, thank God for her life and for the courage and strength you have received from learning about her.

Review your *commitment* to your dream. Celebrate the equation: My Time + My Action = My Success. Prayerfully renew your commitment—to God and to yourself.

You may wonder how you'll be asked to share your dream. *After all,* you may think, *I'm just a novice at this myself. How can I possibly give guidance to anyone else?*

But we have been giving a wonderful gift of discovery to ourselves. We are filled to the brim with information we've gathered. There is no storage place left inside. The only place left for this abundance of knowledge and enthusiasm is outward. To others. To anyone who asks.

When other dreamers (or potential dreamers) discover the information riches within us, they'll want us to share with them the benefits of our experience. And once the pump is primed, it will overflow.

Gladly, we will become a mentor to someone else—just as we were mentored.

Gladly, we will become the friend who will encourage and advise—just as we were encouraged and advised.

Gladly, we will rejoice with the dreamer when her dream is fulfilled and when she becomes a mentor and friend to a new dreamer.

There's an old saying, "Don't repay a kindness; pass it on." Eventually many of us may want to "pass on the kindness" in ways that speak of new dream discoveries that may help any number of people.

When we recall being given a helping hand, a boost into the world of never-before-thought-of dream possibilities, these feelings of "wanting to repay a kindness" are especially acute. Emotions such as gratitude and compassion for others may overflow from within us, unable to be contained.

I am reminded of Martele, a woman I met a few years ago. Martele is an Ethiopian who lives in the United States. With her height and striking good looks, Martele could easily pass for a high fashion model.

Fifteen years ago, Martele's entire family died during the famine that struck her homeland. When the tragic events began to unfold, Martele and her husband Mohammed had just celebrated the birth of their son.

"At first," she told me, "we didn't realize how desperate the situation would become. Ethiopia—all of Africa—experiences droughts from time to time. Things are bad for a while, but then they improve, and life goes on.

"But this was different. Mohammed and I lived on a little farm. There was plenty of food from our crops to feed us and the baby. Until the drought there was always enough seed to plant crops for the next year.

"But when it didn't rain, there was no use planting our seeds; the plants wouldn't live anyway. We became so hungry that we were forced to eat the seeds. When the rains finally came, there was nothing to plant. We had nothing to eat.

"Mohammed decided that we needed to travel to the border, to try to get into a region that hadn't been so devastated by the drought.

"We walked for days. Others walked with us—Mohammed's family and my elderly parents. It seemed that all of us were on the verge of starving. Many were sick and dying. During the night we never knew who we would have to bury in the morning.

"Finally, we reached the border, only to find we would not be allowed to go any further. A refugee camp had been set up for us, and it was filled with thousands of people.

"Illnesses, caused by the unsanitary conditions, swept through families. One night after we had been there only a few weeks Mohammed died from cholera. A few days later, I held our baby in my arms as he took his last breath."

Martele's eyes filled with tears. "I thought that there was nothing left to live for."

I looked at the woman sitting next to me—exquisitely dressed, her eyes warm and animated. It was difficult picturing her in such devastating circumstances.

"What happened?" I asked gently.

"I was found by an Australian nurse, her name was Agnes, who worked for an international relief agency. Agnes took me to the dispensary, gave me medicines and food, nursed me back to health.

"I watched her working with the children, the families, who came to the dispensary. There was such kindness in her face, in her actions.

"One day I asked Agnes why she was giving her life in such a way—I asked her why she wanted to help. She told me that she served a God of love. She told me that he loved me and cared about what happened to me. She said that his heart was broken by my people's suffering. And that he had known my sorrow when Mohammed died and when my baby took his last breath in my arms.

"We talked many times about her God and his Son Jesus. One day I decided I wanted to belong to this God of love, that I wanted to dedicate my life to serving him with the same love and compassion I saw in Agnes. I bowed my head and gave my heart to him.

"Before long I began to share my hopes and dreams with Agnes. I told her about the burning desire in my heart to help others in the world who suffered the way my people were suffering.

"We began to speak of my returning to school and simply opening the door to God's leading. My heart nearly leapt with delight. I knew that this was a dream beyond all I could have hoped or imagined. We prayed together about my dream.

"Agnes made inquiries and eventually arranged for me to come to the United States, live with a family, and attend school."

Martele smiled, her eyes lively. "It wasn't easy, believe me. There were times when I was lonely and sad; other times when pursuing my education seemed so difficult I couldn't go on. But the challenge kept me moving forward. I had known more difficult times than this, and I had lived through them. I would live through this also."

Martele went on to tell me how she had met and married her husband just before graduation from Bible college. Though he was headed toward a degree in business administration, he fully supported her dream of helping disadvantaged people throughout the world.

As soon as Martele graduated she set about beginning her own relief agency. She traveled throughout the United States, speaking in churches and community groups, inspiring others to help her in her efforts.

It took two years to get the funding she needed to begin. She set up a modest office, rolled up her sleeves, and dedicated herself to her dream.

Within another five years, Martele had built her agency into one of the top "gifts-in-kind" relief organizations in the country. Not only did her foundation provide relief supplies to Ethiopia and other African nations during times of crisis, it began working in other countries throughout the world. Following the Gulf War in 1991, it immediately flew in cooking utensils, blankets, and clothing to thousands of Kurdish refugees. In the aftermath of Hurricane Andrew, it provided food and clothing to hundreds of children and families in Florida. And following the devastating Midwest flooding in 1993, Martele's organization donated building supplies to help hundreds of families rebuild their homes.

I asked Martele during our interview why she had chosen this dream to pursue. With her education and model's beauty, she could have pursued a dozen other paths—many of them leading to personal gain and wealth.

She looked thoughtful for a moment, then answered, "So much has been given to me that my heart overflows with that which I want to give back. Even today I just want to repay the kindness that has been shown to me. It simply cannot be any other way."

Martele dared to dream the impossible. I couldn't help but think how her dream will never die. It will live on for generations to come, through the lives of others she has helped throughout the world.

Martele had given—and continues to give—from her inner resources of compassion, joy, perseverance, selflessness, determination. Those things that make up who Martele is today are there in abundance, overflowing, unable to be contained, lovingly and openly shared with others.

I met Josefina in her home in Guatemala City. I was immediately drawn to her friendly, warmhearted manner. There was a spark of immediate kinship, as if we had known each other far longer than just a few minutes.

I had arranged to spend a few hours interviewing Josefina, but before the first hour had passed, she invited me to spend the day with her. Our time together was so delightful that I ended up spending three days in her home and in her community, San Rafael, where she was a leader.

As we began our visit that first day, Josefina and I sat at her kitchen table, munching on a breakfast of warm, homemade tortillas, fresh fruit, and fried pork—a feast for a special guest.

I began asking Josefina about her background, particularly what led to her becoming one of the outstanding leaders in San Rafael.

A serious expression crossed her face as she began telling me the community's history and how her plans and dreams paralleled those of San Rafael.

"San Rafael was completely destroyed in the 1976 Guatemalan earthquake," she began. "My husband and I hadn't been married very long at the time, but we lost everything we had. The house was flattened. The community, as we had known it, was gone.

"A lot of people came in to help us—brought relief supplies at first, then helped us begin rebuilding our homes and businesses.

"I was a young wife and mother, more involved with my family's survival than that of the community, but I never forgot the changes that happened when everyone began working together.

"Life got better for us all. My husband had a good job, and our children were doing well in school. For several years, it seemed that life would just continue on the same path."

Josefina stopped to clear our dishes and to pour coffee. After she had again seated herself, she looked at me, a sadness in her expressive eyes. "That's when our troubles began," she said. "My husband became ill with a crippling arthritis; he lost his job. I had never worked outside the home. We didn't have much savings, and what we did have we used very quickly.

"I've never been so frightened in my life. I even went without food so that my children could eat. I worried that we would lose our home."

"What happened?" I knew that her husband was still unable to work many hours a day.

"My friend Yoli came into my life—and taught me to dream. That's what happened!" Her eyes again turned lively. She laughed. "Yoli had begun her own sewing business in her home to support herself and her daughter. She told me I could do the same thing. I didn't believe her. I had never made anything with my hands before. How could I possibly make anything that people would want to buy?

"But Yoli believed in me. She bought me my first sewing machine, gave me some yardage, and enrolled me in sewing classes. She encouraged me and helped me learn. Next I took a dressmaking class, then a tailoring class. After that I began to create original designs.

"Then I began letting people know I was ready to go into business. I began making dresses for women in the community. A teacher hired me to make thirty-seven graduation robes for her preschool class. I soon made enough money to repay Yoli for the sewing machine. And there was plenty left to buy more supplies and increase my business.

"And all the while I was having a wonderful time. I found this creative side of me that I never knew was there.

"Then some of the other women in the community came to me, asking me to help them learn to sew.

"Me?" she laughed, shaking her head at the incredible thought. "Can you imagine that? Me, a teacher!" She laughed again.

"Then I had a dream. What if I could find a place to hold larger classes for the women? A community center where we could hold classes that would help us all. Not just sewing but other skills that would help us bring in income.

"I got some of the women together. We talked it over and decided to see what we could do. We found a vacant building and talked to the authorities about our plans. They leased it to us for practically nothing."

Josefina grinned. "It was a mess. We had a lot of cleaning up to do before it could be used, but we did it. And it was worth it."

"Josefina," I said. "I'd love to see your community center. Is it far from here?"

"I'd hoped you'd say that," she said. "It's within walking distance. And"—her eyes sparkled—"there's a class going on right now. You can meet some of the other ladies."

We walked to the center, only a few blocks from Josefina's home. Not just one class, but two, were in progress. As we walked through the door, we were greeted by a class of thirty-some exuberant schoolchildren.

I looked at Josefina, surprised.

She laughed. "I forgot to tell you, we've now begun an after-school program for the neighborhood children. Many of them have no place to go if their parents work. They come here for a Bible story and healthy snack. They do crafts and sometimes just play and have a good time."

We then walked to the back of the building where a baking class was in progress. Josefina explained, "These ladies are learning cake decorating. Many of them will be able to find work in bakeries or sell what they make from their homes."

And in a room beyond that, several women were bottling and labeling cosmetics—lotions, creams, shampoos, and conditioners. Josefina saw my quizzical look. "We had a woman, an expert from a cosmetics firm, spend a day with us teaching us to make our own. We work together creating the fragrances and products and then sell them as a group to bring in income for the center."

I was impressed. They had thought of everything!

I spent the next few days getting to know the women, some of whom had formed a community leadership group under Josefina's guidance. I learned that they had a number of concerns about their community. Among them was the plight of girl children in Guatemala. They wanted to do everything in their power to counteract early pregnancy and teen marriage. They wanted to help young women stay in school, gaining education and better skills for the future.

The women have opened their homes and hearts to young women who need help. One thirteen-year-old girl, Melene, is being helped by Josefina. Melene's mother died several years ago. She lives with her grandmother who suffers from Alzheimer's disease. Melene, who calls Josefina her "mama," is learning to sew and receives help and encouragement with her homework.

As I hugged Josefina good-bye at the end of our visit, I couldn't help feeling that I better understood the fulfilled dreamer's need to give from a heart of overflowing gratitude and compassion. I also saw firsthand the vibrant life of a dream that lives on in the lives of those you give it to.

Josefina, with the help of her mentor and friend, Yoli, had first dreamed to help with the immediate needs of her family. Though her initial dream was fulfilled, she didn't stop there. Another dream appeared beyond the horizon, and she rose to the challenge. Not only that, but she enthusiastically encouraged others to help her in her dream for a better community, a better environment in which to raise their families. Josefina chose to dream a dream that will never die.

It will go on living in the lives—the hearts—of those she has touched in San Rafael.

Let's take a look at one more dream that will live through generations to come.

When we last heard of my friend Marihelen, she had completed her first dream: She had graduated from the university with her bachelor's degree in liberal arts. We saw that she dared to dream again, this time completing her master's degree in educational counseling. Then we read that she dared to dream yet again. She was persistently looking to land a job in her field, perhaps the most impossible part of her dream. But knowing my tenacious friend, I knew that this, too, would be achievable.

Nine months (appropriately enough) after Marihelen marched down the aisle in cap and gown and was awarded her M.A., my phone rang.

"Guess what, Sis," she said, reverting to her childhood name for me.

I could hear the excitement in her voice. I couldn't help picturing that little girl I had first met so long ago standing outside my picket fence, ready to show me how to stomp the bees in my patch of clover.

In those days, for Marihelen—that dark-haired, skinny-legged, unafraid-of-anything-looking child—the sheer delight of the whole world had lain open for her to explore. In those days, there had been no doubt about herself, her abilities, or her place in the world. As it should be for children, it was a time of dreaming dreams and of thinking nothing was impossible.

Then, Marihelen's dreams were crushed. She lost confidence in herself, and even the most precious of dreams seemed to lie crumpled somewhere deep inside.

"Well, don't you want to know what my news is?" she laughed, interrupting my thoughts.

"Of course I do!" I exclaimed, though I had an inkling of what was coming.

"It's happened! It's finally happened!"

"You got hired!" I screamed into the phone.

"Yes! Oh, yes!" she said, alternately laughing and crying. "I've been hired to start a counseling program at an elementary school. I'll be working with kids in a gang-infested area, kids who've got all kinds of emotional issues. I get to design the program."

"What do you plan to do?" I asked in awe.

"The kids need to discover that they're loved and valued." She paused, then went on thoughtfully. "They need to see that they've each got special gifts—things that make them special and different from anyone else. Every activity I plan will point to that discovery."

"It's perfect," I said.

"God knew my heart—he knew what was right for me." Her voice, though subdued, was jubilant. "It was worth the wait."

Marihelen fulfilled her third dream, and God helped her fulfill her heart's desire. She began living her dream long before it was fulfilled. Now she dares to help children discover that they too can dream.

Now I await the next telephone call. "Sis," I hear my friend saying to me. "Guess what!"

And I, smiling to myself, will say, "What?"

And she'll say, "Sis, I've got another dream."

I promise I won't say, "I knew that you would someday." I'll just scream into the phone again: "That's wonderful!"

Then I'll settle back and await the news of what Marihelen will dream next.

"The common idea that success spoils people by making them vain, egotistic, and self-complacent is erroneous," Somerset Maugham once said. "On the contrary, it makes them, for the most part, humble, tolerant, and kind. Failure makes people bitter and cruel."

When we succeed in living our dreams, we contribute to the well-being of those around us. We can't help but want to give back (as did Martele, Josefina, and Marihelen) a portion of what was given to us. There is a contagious joy of discovery that will take the form of teaching, mentoring, and coming alongside other dreamers.

Keep your eyes and heart open for opportunities to help others. Listen to their questions. Help them as others have helped you along the road to your dream.

And beyond the individual dreamers who will ask you for advice, look around at your world. How can you, through your dream, make it a better place? Or is there another dream just beyond the horizon that will bring positive change into your world?

Open your thinking to new and maybe radical possibilities that you haven't before considered. In your time of solitude with God, ask how you can make a difference with your gifts and with your dreams.

One hundred years ago, Robert Ingersoll wrote:

My creed is that: Happiness is the only good. The place to be happy is here. The time to be happy is now. The way to be happy is to make others so.

His words are as true today as they were then: Happiness can only be found inside ourselves as we help bring life and love and laughter into others' lives, through shared hopes and dreams.

So share your dreams, dear dreamers.

Let them live forever.


## Being Born Again (It's Not What You Think!)

We opened this book with a scene from the life of a woman whose nest was newly vacated. As her last child left for college, she looked around the empty house, felt an acute loneliness settle in, and sadly wondered, "Who am I?" and, "What will I do with the rest of my life?"

As we've seen in the previous nine chapters, midlife can be a time of tremendous personal growth. We finally have the time to focus on ourselves, to ask in a *positive* way, "What will I do with the rest of my life?"

We've explored the possibilities of dreaming dreams we never before considered.

We've experienced the joy of dream discovery, finding out a little more about who we are and what we'll do with the rest of our lives in the process.

It may have already occurred to you, but if not, consider it now: Midlife is a time of rebirth, emotionally and psychologically. Elizabeth Auchincloss, a psychiatrist at Cornell University Medical College, says that midlife is similar to the time during childhood (at about eighteen months) called *rapprochement* when a child first realizes that she is not omnipotent.

That realization makes the child feel vulnerable for the first time. She responds with a burst of rich personal growth. It is so intense that at least one psychologist has labeled it a second, psychological birth.

At midlife, a woman becomes acutely aware of her own mortality. Her response is nearly the same as it was to the awareness of her vulnerability in early childhood. In fact, according to psychologists, we can think of midlife as a time of giving birth yet again—this time to ourselves.[1]

Giving birth to ourselves?

What an amazing thought!

We just emptied our nests of our children, those little people who grew into bigger people who grew into young adults who finally needed a push to get them airborne.

And what should appear inside the nest: a fledgling self, fresh and new and ready to stretch her wings, perch on the nest's edge, and . . .

Fly.

Because, dear dreamers, that what it's all about: Our dreams, our big dreams, are about flying.

Helen Keller said, "One can never consent to creep when one feels an impulse to soar." After our midlife rebirth we will never again be content to creep. We will dream dreams, and we will soar to heights we never imagined possible.

Let's end this book with the following quotes (and I suggest you write them in your journal). The first from Guillaume Apollinaire:

> "Come to the edge," he said.
> They said, "We are afraid."
> "Come to the edge," he said.
> They came.
> He pushed them . . .
> And they flew.

And Deuteronomy 32:11 (paraphrased):

> He cared for her,
> like an eagle that stirs up its nest
> and hovers over its young,
> that spreads its wings to catch them
> and carries them on its pinions.

~~~
## Reflections

They will soar on wings like eagles.

ISAIAH 40:31

This week—and for the rest of your life—live your dreams. Dare to dream another dream. And another. And yet another. Share your wisdom with other dreamers. Praise the God who created you to take joy in your special dream.

And . . . fly, dear dreamer. Fly.

*Father, you've given us strength for our flight. You've prepared us for soaring. You've brought us to the nest's edge. Carry us on eagles' wings as we fly.*

Listen: there was once a king sitting on his throne. Around him stood great and wonderfully beautiful columns ornamented with ivory, bearing the banners of the king with great honour. Then it pleased the king to raise a small feather from the ground and he commanded it to fly. The feather flew, not because of anything in itself but because the air bore it along. Thus am I . . . a feather on the breath of God.

HILDEGARD OF BINGEN

# Notes

## Chapter 1: There's Finally Time for Me!

1. Barbara Chase-Riboud, *Sallie Hammings*, as quoted by Cathleen Roundtree in *On Women Turning Fifty: Celebrating Mid-Life Discoveries* (San Francisco: Harper San Francisco, 1993), 43.

## Chapter 2: Celebrating Solitude

1. Margery Williams, *The Velveteen Rabbit; or, How Toys Become Real* (Philadelphia: Running Press, 1981), 14–16.
2. Tim Hansel, *Through the Wilderness of Loneliness* (Elgin, Ill.: David C. Cook Publishing Co., 1991), 29.
3. J. I. Packer, *Knowing God* (Downers Grove, Ill.: InterVarsity Press, 1973), 37.

## Chapter 3: It's Okay to Love Ourselves

1. Bill and Gloria Gaither, *I Am a Promise* (Nashville: Word Publishing).
2. "Narcissistic Personalities," in *Diagnostic and Statistical Manual of Mental Disorders*, 3d ed., as cited by David Allen, M.D., *Shattering the Gods Within* (Chicago: Moody Press, 1994), 47.
3. Stephen Johnson, *Humanizing the Narcissistic Style* (New York: Norton Publications, 1987).

## Chapter 4: It's Time to Nurture Ourselves

1. Nutrition information is taken from Paula Brown Doress, et al., *Ourselves Growing Older* (New York: Simon and Schuster, 1987), 51–59.
2. Norman Cousins, "Proving the Power of Laughter," *Psychology Today*, October 1989.
3. Thomas Merton, *Thoughts in Solitude* (New York: Farrar, Straus, and Giroux, 1956), 116.
4. Ibid., 118.
5. *Nave's Topical Bible* (Waco, Tex.: Word Publishers, 1977); Arthur Pink, *The Attributes of God* (Grand Rapids: Baker Book House, 1975); A. W. Tozer, *The Knowledge of the Holy* (San Francisco: Harper and Row, 1961).
6. Laurie Klein, "I Love You, Lord" (Nashville: Maranatha Music, 1978).

## Chapter 5: Expanding the Comfort Zone

1. Bob L. Means, "Chronically Human," as quoted by Tim Hansel, in *Through the Wilderness of Loneliness* (Elgin, Ill: David C. Cook Publishing Co., 1991), 46.

## Chapter 6: Exploring Our Gifts and Discovering Our Purpose

1. Oswald Chambers, *My Utmost for His Highest* (Westwood, N.J.: Barbour and Co., 1963), 347.

## Chapter 9: Committing to Our Dreams

1. W. H. Murray, as quoted by John-Roger and Peter McWilliams in *Do It! Let's Get Off Our Buts* (Los Angeles: Prelude Press, 1991), 286.

## Chapter 10: It's Time to Live Our Dreams!

1. Denise Foley and Eileen Nechas, *Women's Encyclopedia of Health and Emotional Healing* (Emmaus, Pa.: Rodale Press), 5.